Strategic Management

I. Narsis
R. Vani

Published by

7/22, Ansari Road, Darya Ganj, New Delhi-110002
Phones : +91-11-40775252, 23273880, 23275880, 23280451
Fax: +91-11-23285873
Web: www.atlanticbooks.com
E-mail: orders@atlanticbooks.com

Branch Office
5, Nallathambi Street, Wallajah Road, Chennai-600002
Phones : +91-44-64611085, 32413319
E-mail: chennai@atlanticbooks.com

Printed in India at Nice Printing Press, A-33/3A, Site-IV, Industrial Area, Sahibabad, Ghaziabad, U.P.

Preface

In a few words, we would like to revisit the fundamental question: Why did we write the book in the first place? After all, there are already some strategy textbooks available. This is because we felt that there was a need for a book that students would find both relevant and readable, but at the same time challenging.

The aim of this book is to provide a concise presentation of the theory and practice of strategic management, with particular emphasis on effective, responsive strategy-making processes. The scope is comprehensive and research-based and yet presents the content in an accessible manner, ready to be applied in management practice. The book presents conventional and newer tools for practical strategy analysis and considers the associated strategy process expressed in an integrative strategy model, where strategic responsiveness is a necessary precursor for organizational adaptation.

These themes are anchored in the core elements of strategic management, together with inputs from current research efforts. Hence, the book can be used as a general strategy textbook in contemporary MBA programs where there is a need for a succinct overview of the field. By adding selected reference articles and related case studies, it can form a solid base for graduate classes in strategic management. It may also serve as a useful foundation for different executive programs where participants want to probe the strategy field, challenge their current thinking, and consider approaches to effective strategy making that can be applied to their own organizations. With a general grounding in the strategy literature, including key references, it might even serve as a useful core text for Ph.D. students with a general interest in the strategic management field.

We have endeavored to use an engaging writing style, free of unnecessary jargon, to cover all the traditional bases, and to integrate some central themes throughout the book that are vital to understanding strategic management in today's global economy. Among these themes are globalization, technology, ethics, and entrepreneurship.

I. Narsis
R. Vani

Contents

Chapter 1

Business Policy

1.1 INTRODUCTION

Policy making is one of the important components of business planning. Existence of every organization is based on its policy making and implementing capabilities. Business policy refers to decision about the future of ongoing enterprise. These are the decisions taken by top management of the enterprise having investigating market opportunities, competence of the enterprise and potential resources to extract the available opportunities.

It involves the choice of purpose, the moulding of organizational identity and character, the continuous definition of what needs to be done, and the mobilization of resources for the attainment of goals.

It involves setting long-term objectives which will guide the destiny of enterprise.

Business policy helps in deciding on manpower, capital, plant and equipments, materials needed to achieve the objectives.

1.2 EVOLUTION OF BUSINESS POLICY

Year	Institution	Recommendations
1911	Harvard Business School	Introduced a course in "Management" in order to impact instructions to students to increase the management capability.
1959	Ford Foundation	Business policy provides an opportunity for students "to pull together what they have learned in separate business fields and utilize this knowledge in the analysis of complex business problems".

1969	American Assembly of Collegiate schools of Business	Business policy as a mandatory requirement for the purpose of recognition
1990	All India Council of Technical Education (AICTE)	Business policy as an integrative component in the management studies curriculum, in the form of Corporate Planning and Strategic Management.

1.3 MEANING OF POLICY

The term policy is derived from Greek word "*politeia*" relating to polity and the Latin word "*polotis*" which means polished, that is to clear.

A policy is a broad guideline for decision-making that links the formulation of strategy with its implementation. Companies use policies to make sure that employees throughout the firm make decisions and take actions that support corporate's mission, objectives and strategies.

1.4 DEFINITIONS

- "Policies are strategic guidelines for action. They spell out what can and what cannot to be done in all areas of a company's operation."—*Robert J. Mockler*
- "Managements expressed or implied intent to govern action in the achievement of company's aims".
- "A policy is a statement or general understanding which provides guidance in decision-making to members of an organization in respect to any course of action".

1.5 NATURE OF BUSINESS POLICY

As already observed, policies are basically formulated by the management or the general management for guiding, directing and facilitating the thinking and acting process of the various functional executives, to ensure the best contribution towards the corporate objectives and goals. Policy can either is formal or informal, which can be applied, implied or imposed.

It originates from the top management for the express purpose of guiding themselves and their subordinates to make use of their operational tools as effectively as possible. It also enables to set objectives for the whole organization in general and for the various functional areas in particular.

It is the corporate policy that creates a sense of mission and purpose in the executive value judgement, and in their managerial operations, because a direct and purposeful preparation to face the challenges, opportunities and threats of the day-to-day business activities, is provided by the business policy from time to time.

According to Edmund, the associates' business policy is concerned with the top management function of:

1. Shaping high-level, long-range corporate objectives and strategies that will be matched, to both company capacities and to external realities in a world market by rapid technological, economic, social and political change.
2. Casting up an effective well-matched set of general policies for the pursuit of that strategy.
3. Guiding the organization in accordance with that strategy.

The mission of the top management is influenced by the policy at various levels and phases. They are:

1. Perception of industry and economic trends that affect the prospects of the economy.
2. Clearly understanding the needs, opportunities, threats, strengths, weakness and problems.
3. Selecting the best opportunity or opportunities from an array of them, this can cope with the capacity of the company.
4. Formulating of a strategy taking into account the opportunity and availability of resources.
5. Development of operating plans for the pursuit of the chosen strategy and policies.
6. Creation of organizational relationships, organizational climate, and an atmosphere for the proper implementation of policy.
7. Evaluating the performance and the progress.

8. Periodic re-evaluation of positions in the light of developments within the organization and its environment.

To sum up it can observe that the overall performance of the company depends on the pragmatic policies, and the top management is mainly responsible for the policy formulation.

Business policies cover such a wide variety of subjects and are so broad-based that every possible matter that affects the interests of any one in the organization, the community and the government are included in them.

In fact, business policies cover all the functional areas of business-production, marketing, personnel and finance. These functional areas are generally covered by the term as "major policies" and "minor policies".

1.6 SCOPE OF POLICY

No business organization can survive or grow without definite objectives. These objectives can be accomplished by applying different policies from time to time depending upon the environment. Business policies are the guidelines for organizational thinking, behavior and action. Policies are formulated pertaining to different aspects of an organization and therefore they enjoy a very wide concept. Persons concerned with any type of activity will have to think of clear-cut policies right from the formulation stage to the winding up of the organization. Scope of the business policy should be linked with the different functional areas of business units.

Policy in general, are concerned with:

1. Aims and objectives of a business unit.
2. Organizational Structure.
3. Financial resources available.
4. Personnel problems relating to recruitment, promotion, retirement, compensation, etc.
5. Regional tradition and social values.
6. Fiscal and commercial policy of the government.
7. Government regulations and controls.

Thus policies cover a wide range of subjects and are therefore having a broad-based scope from formation to winding-up of the business organization.

1.7 PARAMETERS OF POLICY

There are certain parameters for business policy, they are:

1. Policy should be identifiable and clear, either in words or in practice.
2. Objectives of the policy should be fully identified and well defined.
3. Policy should not be conflicting with other functional and divisional policies of the company.
4. The policy should be capable enough to fully exploit the opportunities.
5. Policy should be characterized by fairness and honesty with organizational philosophy, objectives, goals and strategy.
6. Policy should be appropriate to the desired level of contribution to society.
7. Policy should be acceptable to all concerned, i.e., it should be appropriate to the personal values and aspirations of the key managers.
8. Policy should constitute a clear stimulus to organizational effort and commitment.
9. Policy should always be realistic.

1.8 IMPORTANCE OF BUSINESS POLICY

Business policies play a dominant role in managing an enterprise in an effective manner. Business policy is important for the following reasons:

1. Solving Business Problems

Policies are formed for solving varied business problems. In the absence of well-defined policies, the manager is handicapped in respect of running the company smoothly and successfully. Policies help managers to solve problems by taking prompt decisions and quick action.

2. Policies Provide Stability

Business policy provides certainty of action. Modifications are made to the existing policies depending upon the changed environment. Hence, policies provide perpetual continuity and promote stability organization. This results in avoiding frustration among members of the organization.

3. Policies helps Manager to Improve his Managerial Powers

Policies helps manager to improve his managerial powers. He can guide his subordinates through decisions taken in accordance with the policies from time to time even though subordinates will enable the manager to control and govern the subordinates without visiting their offices. This will further help the manager to devote more time to executions such as planning, organizing, directing, controlling.

4. Helps in Administration

Policies helps the individuals of different operational areas are properly guided. This avoids the duplication of works. Policy establishes good co-ordination between the people working in the organization. Well drafted policy helps subordinates to act with full liberty within the framework of the policies adopted.

5. Optimum Utilization of Resources

Polices help in avoiding wastages. Policies specify the limit and extent of the organizational resources. This will certainly guide individuals to use the allotted resources optimally.

6. Ensure Consistency

Policies are control guides of delegated decision-making. They seek to ensure consistency and uniformity in decisions on problems that recur frequently and under similar, but not identical circumstances.

7. Policies Serve as a Yardstick for Measuring the Performance

Policies provide specific routes towards selected goals. This serves as a standard for evaluating performance. The actual results can be compared with the policies to know the extent to which the goals have been achieved.

8. Creation of Goodwill

Corporate policies built up an image of the business in the eyes of the public and this brings in more reputation, goodwill, and profit so that more and more socially responsible activities can be undertaken.

1.9 FEATURES OF POLICY

Various features of business policy are as follows:

1. **Clear Guidelines.** Policies provide *clear guidelines* to the members in the organization for deciding a course of action. By this, the freedom of the members of the organization in choosing the course of action is restricted. From this point of view policies are quite important in role theory. Policies explain what organization members should do as contrast to what they are doing. Policies when enforced permit prediction of roles with certainty not end in themselves, but means to ends in business.
2. **Expressed in Qualitative and Conditional Manner.** Generally policies are expressed in a qualitative and conditional manner by using verbal expressions like 'to maintain', 'to provide', 'to assist', 'to assure', 'to produce', 'to convince', etc. Such prescriptions may be either explicit or they may be interpreted from the behavior of organization members, particularly those at the top level.
3. **Act as a Function to Manager.** Policy formulation is a function of all the managers in an organization, as some form of guideline is required at every level for future course of action. However, the higher the level of a manager, the more important is his role in policy making.
4. **Achieving Objectives.** Finally, a policy is formulated in the context of organizational objectives. Therefore, the policy tries to contribute towards the achievement of organizational objectives.

1.10 PURPOSE OF BUSINESS POLICY

Here we can know the main purposes of business policy:

1. **Clarity of Objectives.** Policies guide action to accomplish the pre-determined objectives. Policies are inseparable from objectives and hence they are linked with objectives. Policies provide a clear idea regarding the area of application and proper decisions are taken in such areas.
2. **Proper Guidance.** Policy establishes the parameters within which the strategic decisions are taken. It directs overall action for the achievement of the objectives.
3. **Helps in Decision-making.** Policy play a crucial role in helping the subordinates to be creative and innovative in solving the problems. Employees can take quick decisions within the parameters of the policy. This leads to operational decisions.
4. **Facilitates Coordination and Control.** Business policy provides powerful mechanism which will guide the general direction of action and decisions. Through policies, the efforts of organizational members can be interrelated so that they work as a cohesive unit.
5. **Yardstick for Evaluating Action:** Policies act as a yardstick for evaluating the overall quality of executive decision-making and action. Actual performance can easily be compared with the pre-defined policies to ascertain the deviations.
6. **Ensure Consistency and Uniformity:** Policy seeks to achieve consistency and uniformity. Stable policy inspires confidence in the minds of the employees, customers and other related people.

1.11 PYRAMID OF BUSINESS POLICY

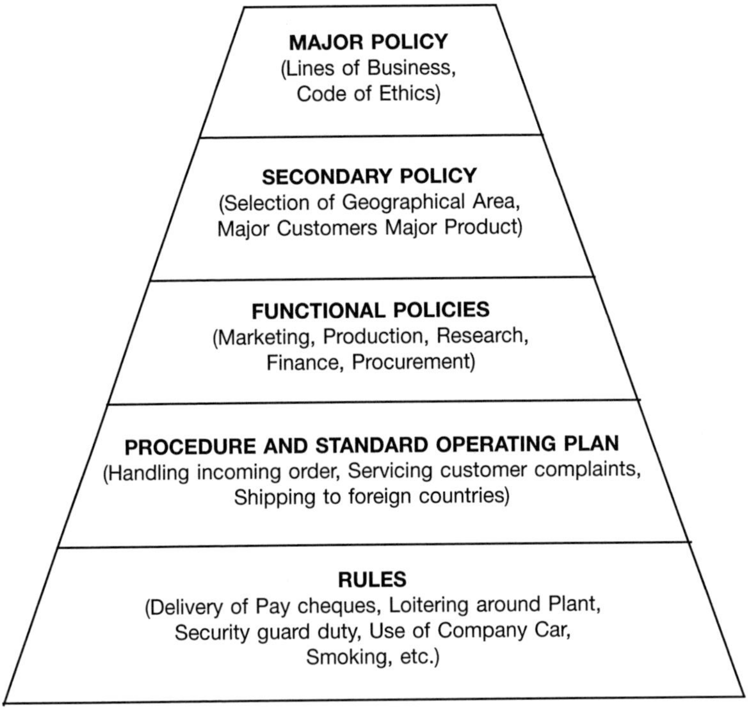

MAJOR POLICY
(Lines of Business,
Code of Ethics)

SECONDARY POLICY
(Selection of Geographical Area,
Major Customers Major Product)

FUNCTIONAL POLICIES
(Marketing, Production, Research,
Finance, Procurement)

PROCEDURE AND STANDARD OPERATING PLAN
(Handling incoming order, Servicing customer complaints,
Shipping to foreign countries)

RULES
(Delivery of Pay cheques, Loitering around Plant,
Security guard duty, Use of Company Car,
Smoking, etc.)

Chapter 2

Strategic Management

2.1 VALUE OF STRATEGIC MANAGEMENT

The complex and sophisticated business environment has created an urgent need for strategic management for organizations. To deal effectively with the challenges of environment, including competitors, when profits are at stake; suppliers, when resources are becoming even more scarce; government agencies when adherence to growing number of regulations has become imperative and customers, who have more and more expectations from the products in the form of quality, service, cost and delivery to their satisfaction. Companies are designing strategic management process to adequately account for all these variables.

The strategic management process facilitate to optimally position a firm in a given competitive environment. The positioning of the companies in environment that is charged with competition is quite accurately done using strategic management process, as it permits more realistic and accurate assessment of anticipated environmental changes and gear the organization for being proactive to predatory competition. The strategic management process also ensures preparedness of the companies to unexpected internal or external pressures and sustains them.

2.2 MEANING OF STRATEGIC MANAGEMENT

The strategic management or strategic planning encompasses long range plans, new venture management, planning, programming, budgeting, business policy, etc. with greater emphasis on environmental scanning and forecasting and taking into account external and internal factors in formulating and implementing the plans.

Today, strategic management is understood as a process of formulating objectives of an organization and developing methods to achieve them. It is a process of designing a path and selecting one path, after due to evaluation of various alternatives for reaching a goal. The objective can be in the form of a mission statement or may be clearly defined in the form of postulates.

Strategic management is a science of choosing the alternatives from the designed and available courses. The manager have to decide on a process that will be most suitable to their conditions and that would enable them to achieve a desired position of their organization.

The word strategy is derived from the Greek Word "Strategia" that was evolved during 400 BC. The word Strategia means science of guiding and directing military forces.

2.3 DEFINITION OF STRATEGIC MANAGEMENT

- "Strategic management is concerned with making decisions about an organization's future direction and implementing those decisions."—*Lloyd L. Byars*
- "The pattern of objectives for achieving these goals and the major policies and plans for achieving these goals stated in such a way so as to define what business the company is in or is to be and the kind of company it is or it is to be."—*Andrews*
- "Strategy can be defined as the determination of basic long-term objectives of an enterprise had the adoption of courses of action and the allocation of resources for carrying out of these goals."—*Chandler*

2.4 NEED FOR STRATEGIC MANAGEMENT

A company's strategy provides a central purpose and direction to the activities of the organization. Company must employ strategies to accomplish its basic objectives. These strategies must be clearly communicated to the people working in the organization.

1. Due to Changing Environment

Every organization is linked with the external environment which is always subject to changes. Hence, strategic management act as a tool for the top management executives to forecast the changes well in advance and to take the advantage of the various opportunities available to overcome the various risks.

2. Provide Guidelines

Strategic decision is the basis for the formulation of sub strategies. Operational strategies are formulated based on the strategic decisions. Strategic decision provides a framework within which all other supporting decision should be formulated.

3. Better Performance

Strategic policy is always related to the better and efficient use of the various strategic decisions. Businesses which plan strategically have the scope of higher probability of success.

4. Better Allocation of Resources

Strategic management paves the way for better allocation of resources of an organization. It helps the management to alter the strategic decisions according to the changing environment and allot the resources accordingly.

5. Competitive Advantage

Strategic management aims at gaining sustainable competitive edge for the firm. It helps in evaluating the competitive environment of the various organizations and exploits the available opportunities.

6. Increasing Rate of Changes

The environment in which the business operates is fast and changing. A business concern which does not keep its policies up to date, cannot survive for a long-time in the competitive market. In turn, the efficiency strategy optimizes profits over a long-run.

7. Higher Motivation of Employees

The employees are designed clear cut duties by the top management, viz. what is to be done, who is to do, how to do it, and when to do it? It helps the employees to become loyal, sincere and goal oriented and their efficiency is also increased.

They also get rewards and promotions resulting in higher motivation for the employees. A strategy must respect the human values and duly consider the aspirations of individual members.

8. Strategic Decision-making

Under strategic planning, the first step is to set the goals or objectives of a business concern. Strategic decisions taken under strategic management help the smooth sailing of an enterprise. Strategic planning is the overall planning of operations for the effective implementation of policies.

9. Optimization of Profits

An effective strategy should develop from policies of a concern. It takes into account the various actions of the competitors. It considers future operations in respect of market area and opportunity, executive competence, available resources and limitations imposed by the government. An effective strategy should optimize the profits for the long-run.

2.5 EVOLUTION OF STRATEGIC MANAGEMENT

Till 1930s most firms were happy focusing attention on their day to day, short-term activities. In an environment characterised by very little competition, a functional orientation supported by budgeting and control systems guided the fortunes of firms. The ad hoc policy making yielded ground to planned policy formulation.

In 1940, the emphasis shifted to the integration of functional areas in the context of environmental demands.

The period of 1960s and 1980s, was characterised by rapid environmental changes and increased complexity of business functions necessitating long-range planning and comprehensive business policies aimed at placing a firm in an advantageous relationship to its environment.

During early 1990s, interest in the role of strategy in building competitive advantage resulted in a shift of interest towards the internal aspects of the firm. Strategic management is currently the core of the business policy discipline everywhere.

Summarised Format for Evolution of Strategic Management

Period	1950s	1960s	1970s	Late 1970s to early 1980s	Late 1980s to early 1990s	Mid to late 1990s
Dominant Theme	Budgetary Planning and Control	Corporate planning	Corporate strategy	Analysis of industry and competition	The Quest of Competitive advantage	Strategic Innovation
Main Issues	Financial control through operating budgets	Planning growth	Portfolio planning	Choice of industries, markets and segments and positioning with them	Sources of competitive advantage within the firm	Strategic and Organizational advantage
Principal Concepts and Techniques	Financial Budgeting, Investment planning, Project Appraisal	Forecasting investment planning models	Synergy SBUs Portfolio planning matrices, Experience curves Returns to market share	Analysis of industry structure, competitor analysis—PIMS Analysis	Resource Analysis, Analysis of Core competence	Dynamic source of competitive advantage, Control of Standards, Knowledge and Learning
Organizational implications	Financial management the key	Rise of corporate planning departments and five year formal plans	Diversification, multidivisional structures, Quest for global market share	Greater Industry and Market Selectivity. Industry restructuring, Active Asset Management	Corporate restructuring and business process reengineering, Refocusing and outsourcing	The Virtual Organization, The Knowledge based firm, Alliances and networks, The quest for critical mass

2.6 NATURE OF STRATEGIC MANAGEMENT

Strategic management is well-organised approach that is based on the effective principles and process of management to recognize the corporate objective or mission of business. It establishes suitable target to assure the objectives, identify existing opportunities and restraints in the environment, and develop a logical realistic process to accomplish company objectives.

Strategic management is both the process and beliefs to determine and control the organizational affiliation in its vibrant environment. It is a process to describe approaches and procedures to help management become accustomed to the current business environment through the use of objectives and strategies. As a philosophy, it changes the viewpoint of manager to deal with competitors, customers, and markets and even the organization itself. Its purpose is to motivate management wakefulness of the strategic implication of environmental events and internal decisions.

2.7 SCOPE OF STRATEGIC MANAGEMENT

Strategic management is both an Art and Science of formulating, implementing and evaluating, cross-functional decisions that facilitate an organization to accomplish its objectives. The purpose of strategic management is to use and create new and different opportunities for future. The nature of strategic management is dissimilar form other factors of management as it demands awareness to the "big picture" and a rational assessment of the future options. It offers a strategic direction endorsed by the team and stakeholders, a clear business strategy and vision for the future, a method for accountability and a structure for governance at the different levels, a logical framework to handle risk in order to guarantee business continuity.

The capability to exploit opportunities and react to external change by ongoing strategic decisions.

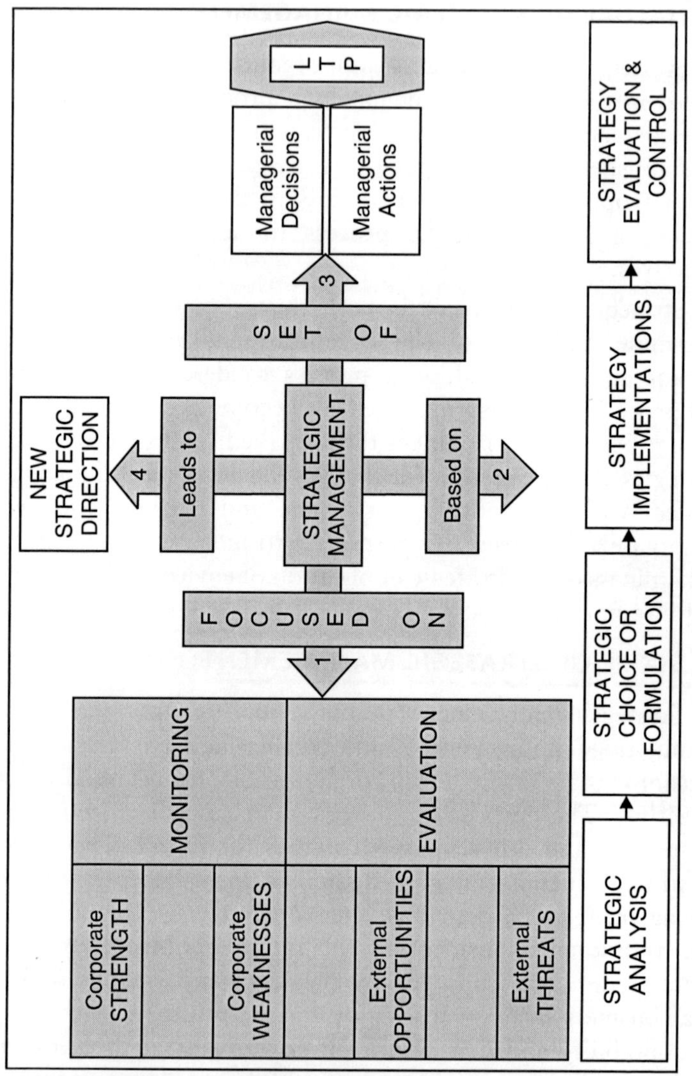

2.8 MODES OF STRATEGIC MANAGEMENT

Modes of strategic management are the approaches adopted by managers in formulating and implementing strategies. They address the issues of who has the major influence in the strategic management process and how the process is carried out.

Managers generally use one of the three major approaches to strategic management: entrepreneurial, adaptive and planning.

Entrepreneurial Mode

In the entrepreneurial mode, strategy is developed mainly by a strong visionary chief executive who actively searches for new opportunities, is heavily oriented toward growth and is willing to make bold decisions or to shift strategies whenever necessary.

The entrepreneurial mode is generally found in organizations that are young or small, have a strong leader or are in such serious trouble that bold moves are their only hope. The vision and dynamism of the top leaders, who enjoy absolute power, shape the future of the organization.

Adaptive Mode

This is an approach to strategy formulation that emphasis taking small, incremental steps reacting to problems rather than seeking opportunities and attempting to satisfy a number of organizational power groups. The adaptive mode is characterized thus, by some familiar features:

1. The focus is on solving problems of immediate concern, rather than developing long-term strategies.
2. Instead of meeting problems head-on in a bold way, the executives try to follow a reactive approach.
3. This approach is used by managers in established organizations that face a rapidly changing environment and yet several coalitions or power blocks, that make it difficult to obtain agreement on clear strategic goals and associated long-term plans (Mintzberg).
4. The emphasis is on taking small, incremental steps aimed at appraising powerful coalitions within the organization. Since power gets distributed it is always not possible to develop major goals, take bold initiatives and get ahead in a unified way.

Planning Mode

This is an approach to strategy formulation that involves systematic, comprehensive analysis along with the integration of various decisions and strategies. The aim of the planning mode is to understand the environment well enough to influence it.

It is most commonly used in large organizations that have enough resources to conduct detailed analysis, have an internal situation where agreement can be reached on major goals, and operate in an environment that has enough stability to enable the formulation and implementation of carefully conceived strategies.

2.9 ADVANTAGES OF STRATEGIC MANAGEMENT

Following are the advantages of strategic management:

1. Discharges Responsibility

Many organization undertake a strategic management process in order to discharge their responsibilities. There is an expectation from shareholders, stakeholders and the general community at large, that a well-managed organization has a strategic management process that guides its future success.

2. Allows an Objective Assessment

Strategic management provides a discipline that allows the senior management team to take a step back from day to day business and think about the future of the organization. Without this discipline, the organization can become solely consumed with working through the next issue or problem without consideration to the larger picture, longer-term trends associated operational and environmental alignment.

3. Provides a Framework for Decision-making

It is not possible (nor realistic or appropriate), for senior management to know all the operational decisions made on day to day business. The cumulative effect of these day to day decisions can have an impact on the success of the organization. Providing a framework within which staff can make the decisions better focused on their efforts on those activities that will support the organizational goals.

4. Enables Understanding and Buy-in

Participation in strategic management process enables better understanding of the direction, why that direction has chosen, and their associated benefits. Establishing the right process for the formulation and communication of strategy not only allows thinking that challenges the status but build support for developed solution. Good strategy formulation and communication process are the key steps in enabling effective and efficient strategy deployment.

5. Enables Measures of Progress

A strategic management process forces an organization to set objectives and measures of success. The setting of measures of success requires that the organization, first determine what is critical to its ongoing success and then forces the establishment of objectives and keeps these critical measures in front of the board and senior management.

6. Provides an Organizational Perspective

Addressing operational issues rarely looks at the whole organization and the interrelatedness of its varying components. Strategic management takes an organizational perspective and looks at all the components and the interrelationship between those components in order to develop a strategy that is optimal for the whole organization.

2.10 RISK OF STRATEGIC MANAGEMENT

Whenever a process is formalized, bureaucratic burden condition is functioning in an organization. This stifles creativity, innovation, and new knowledge that may otherwise be free. There is a risk of losing track of primary objectives for which the entire activity was started and get lost in the bureaucratic jungle of hierarchy.

Repetitive and Time Consuming

Strategic management is repetitive and time consuming activity and managers may soon lose interest due to monotony. The entire activity may start with a big bang and with an exhilarating challenges, creating lot of enthusiasm and commitment but soon, this may fade away and what would be left is a bureaucratic routine.

Frustrations and Disappointment

The managers may become frustrated and disappointed due to unattained expectations and hence they must be trained to anticipate, minimize, and constructively deal with situations. Managers misunderstand that their association and acceptance of their plans will fetch them all the associated rewards. Managers must be trained to negate such expectations, as success may raise their expectations too high and failures may make them feel highly frustrated.

1. Need of permits and industrial licenses that resulted in a set back to entrepreneurship and initiative to people due to wide spread corruptive practices that had taken roots. The government undertakings in some cases were forced to sell goods at prices lower than the cost price. The business environment lacked competition.
2. Emphasis on self-reliance, thus making the Indian Industry insulated from the world. Wide spread eruptions of manufacturing units that made crude products, copying designs of communist countries because it was easier for them.
3. The investment were that disproportionate to their needs and hence uneconomical and self-defeating systems came into being.
4. Large investments in public enterprises without accountability and autonomy that led to monopolies.
5. Spiraling taxation structure lead to evolution of parallel economy. The tax evasions were of a very high magnitude.

2.11 HIERARCHICAL LEVELS OF STRATEGY

Strategy can be formulated on three different levels:

1. Corporate level
2. Business unit level
3. Functional (or) Departmental level

While strategy may be about competing and surviving as a firm, one can argue that products, not corporation compete, and products are developed by business units. The role of the corporation is to manage its business units and products so that each is competitive and so that each contributes to corporate purpose.

Corporate Level Strategy

Corporate level strategy provides the overall direction in terms of its general attitude towards growth and management of business. Typically they fit in three main categories of stability, growth and retrenchment.

Business Level Strategy

Business level strategy is the strategy followed at the business unit or product level. It normally aims at improving the competitive position in the market served by that business unit.

Functional Level Strategy

Functional level strategy refers to the approach in a functional area to achieve corporate and business unit objectives. It is concerned with the development of a distinctive competence to provide an organization or a business unit with competitive advantage.

LEVELS OF STRATEGY

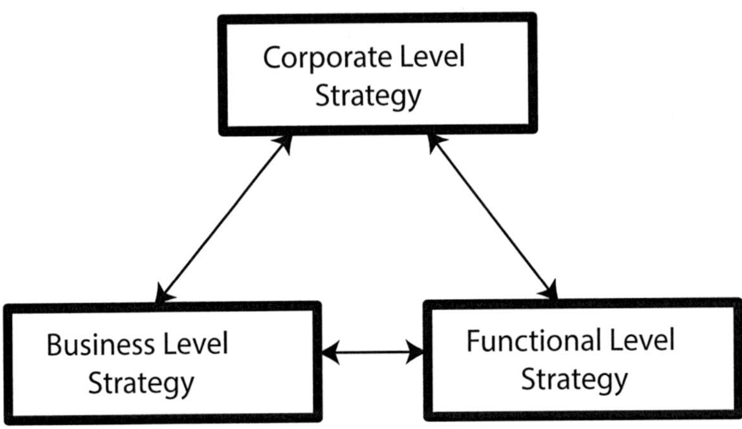

Chapter 3

Strategic Decision-Making

Strategic management is characterized by its emphasis on strategic decision-making. As an organization grows bigger and become complex with high degree of uncertainty, decision-making also become complicated and difficult. Strategic decision have to deal essentially with the long-term future of the organization.

A Chief Executive Officer (CEO) is the Principal Strategist, others include the Board of Directors, Line Managers, Staff Assistants to CEO, Corporate Planners, Public Relations Advisors, Legal Officers, responsible for an organization overall direction, success (or) failure.

The CEO must analyze and seek the answers for the various criteria like:

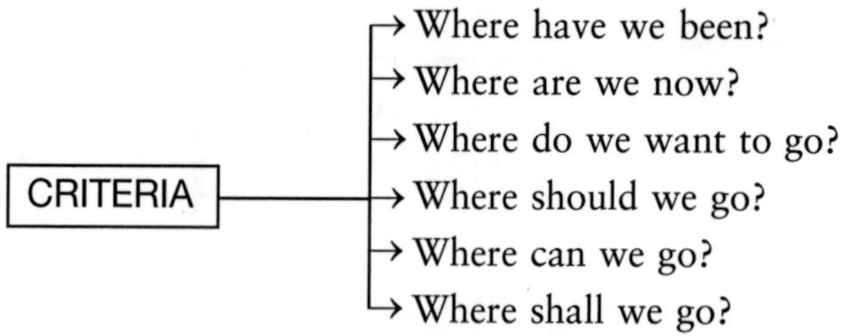

3.1 CHARACTERISTICS OF STRATEGIC DECISION-MAKING

The following are the characteristics of the strategic decision-making:

1. Rare

Strategic decision-making are not common and have no precedents.

2. Consequential

Strategic decision-making involves committing substantial resources of the company and hence a high degree of commitment from persons at all levels.

3. Directive

Strategic decision can serve as precedents for less important decisions and future actions of the organization.

3.2 STRATEGIC DECISION-MAKING PROCESS

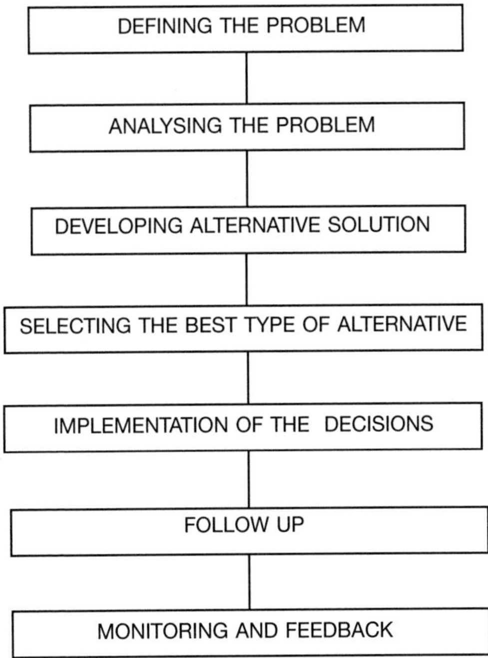

Decision-making is concerned with the selection of one alternative course of action from two or more alternative courses of action.

Precisely it can be stated as a choice-making activity.

These steps can be explained as under:

1. Define the Problem

The first and the foremost step in the decision-making process are to define the real problem. A problem can be explained as a question for and appropriate solution. The manager should consider critical or strategic factors in defining the problem. These factors are, in fact, obstacles in the way of finding proper solution. These are also known as limiting factors.

For example, if a machine stops working due to non-availability of screw, screw is the limiting factor in this case.

2. Analysing the Problem

After defining the problem, the next important step is a systematic analysis of the available data. Sound decisions are based on proper collection, classification and analysis of facts and figures.

There are three principles relating to the analysis and classification as explained below:

(i) The futurity of the decision. This means to what length of time, the decision will be applicable to a course of action.

(ii) The impact of decision on other functions and areas of the business.

(iii) The qualitative considerations which come into the picture.

3. Developing Alternative Solutions

After defining and analysing the problem, the next step is to develop alternative solutions. The main aim of developing alternative solutions is to have the best possible decision out of the available alternative courses of action. In developing alternative solutions the manager comes across creative or original solutions to the problems.

In modern times, the techniques of operations research and computer applications are immensely helpful in the development of alternative courses of action.

4. Selecting the Best Type of Alternative

After developing various alternatives, the manager has to select the best alternative. It is not an easy task.

The following are the four important points to be kept in mind in selecting the best from various alternatives:

(a) Risk element involved in each course of action against the expected gain.

(b) Economy of effort involved in each alternative, i.e. securing desired results with the least efforts.

(c) Proper timing of the decision and action.

(d) Final selection of decision is also affected by the limited resources available at our disposal. Human resources are always limited. We must have right type of people to carry out our decisions. Their calibre, understanding, intelligence and skill will finally determine what they can and cannot do.

5. Implementation of the Decision

Under this step, a manager has to put the selected decision into action.

For proper and effective execution of the decision, three things are very important, i.e.,

(a) Proper and effective communication of decisions to the subordinates. Decisions should be communicated in clear, concise and understandable manner.

(b) Acceptance of decision by the subordinates is important. Group participation and involvement of the employees will facilitate the smooth execution of decisions.

(c) Correct timing in the execution of decision minimizes the resistance to change. Almost every decision introduces a change and people are hesitant to accept a change. Implementation of the decision at the proper time plays an important role in the execution of the decision.

6. Follow up

A follow up system ensures the achievement of the objectives. It is exercised through control. Simply stated it is concerned with the process of checking the proper implementation of decision. Follow up is indispensable so as to modify and improve upon the decisions at the earliest opportunity.

7. Monitoring and Feedback

Feedback provides the means of determining the effectiveness of the implemented decision. If possible, a mechanism should be built which would give periodic reports on the success of the implementation. In addition, the mechanisms should also serve as an instrument of "preventive maintenance", so that the problems can be prevented before they occur.

According to Peter Drucker, the monitoring system should be such that the manager can go and look for himself for first hand information which is always better than the written reports or other second-hand sources. In many situations, however, computers are very successfully used in monitoring since the information retrieval process is very quick and accurate and in some instances the self-correcting is instantaneous.

Strategic Management Process

Strategic management approach entails the following phases:

4.1 STEP LADDER APPROACH OF STRATEGIC MANAGEMENT PROCESS

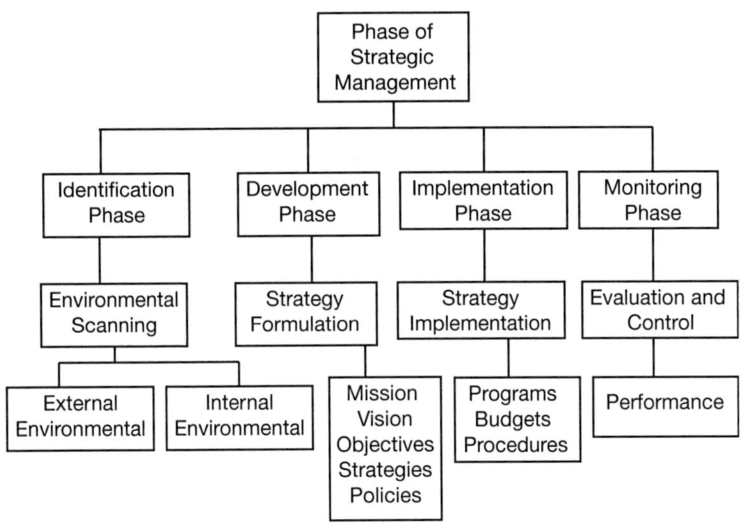

4.1(a) *IDENTIFICATION PHASE*

Environmental Scanning

Environmental scanning is the monitoring, evaluating and disseminating of information from the external and internal environment to key people within the organization.

(a) *External Environment*

The strategic manager must first be aware of the many variable within the corporate societal and task environment. It includes those elements (or) groups that directly affect the corporation and in turn affected by it. The various groups are as follows:

- Government
- Local Community
- Supplier
- Competitor
- Customers
- Creditors
- Employees

External environment comprises of:

Societal Environment. It includes general forces that do not directly touch on the short run activities of the organization, and influences on long run decisions.

Economic Forces. It regulate the exchange of materials, money, energy and information.

Technological Forces. It generates problem-solving inventions.

Political and Legal Forces. It helps to allocate power and provide constraining and protecting laws and regulations.

Socio-cultural Forces. It helps to regulate the values, money, and customs of the society.

(b) *Internal Environment*

The conditions, entities, events and factors within an organization that influences its activities and choices, particularly the behavior of the employees. Factors that are frequently considered as a part of the internal environment are:

- Organization Mission
- Leadership Style
- Organizational Culture.

For a strategy to succeed, it should be based on a realistic assessment of the firm's internal resources and capabilities. An internal analysis provides the means to identify the strengths to build on and the weaknesses to overcome when formulating strategies. The internal analysis process considers the firm's resources; the business the firm is in; its objectives; and plans; and how well they were achieved.

All organizations irrespective of their size, nature, and scope of business perform the functions of finance, production, marketing, and human resource development. For efficient strategic management, careful planning, execution, and coordination of various functions are essential.

Each of the functional areas has strengths or weaknesses depending on how the function is being managed. The joint performance of these functions will have a direct bearing on the firm's performance in terms of superior product design and quality, superior customer service, and superior speed.

4.1(b) *DEVELOPMENT PHASE*

Strategy Formulation

Formulating strategies involves determining appropriate courses of action for achieving objectives. This part deals primarily with the strategy formulation process. The process of strategy formulation begins with analysis with the principal factors in a firm's internal and external environment and ends with functional strategies designed. It also includes such activities as analysis, planning and selecting mission, objectives, and corporate and business strategies. As discussed in the following six chapters, strategy formulation combines a future-oriented perspective with concern for a firm's internal and external environment in developing its competitive plan of action.

(a) *Mission*

A written declaration of an organization's core purpose and focus that normally remains unchanged over time. Properly crafted mission statements

(1) serve as filters to separate what is important from what is not

(2) clearly state which markets will be served and how

(3) communicate a sense of intended direction to the entire organization.

A mission is different from a vision in that the former is the cause and the latter is the effect; a mission is something to be accomplished whereas a vision is something to be pursued for that accomplishment.

(b) *Objectives*

Business goals and objectives are part of the planning process. They describe what a company expects to accomplish throughout the year. Business owners usually outline their goals and objectives in their business plans. These goals and objectives might pertain to the company as a whole, departments, employees, customers and even marketing efforts. Most companies use specific measurements to keep track of their goals and objectives.

(c) *Strategies*

A method or plan chosen to bring about a desired future, such as achievement of a goal or solution to a problem.

The art and science of planning and marshalling resources for their most efficient and effective use. The term is derived from the Greek word for generalship or leading an army.

Business strategy focus on improving competitive positions of a company (or) business units products (or) services within specific industry or market segments that the company serves. Strategy may be competitive (or) co-operative.

(d) *Policies*

A set of policies are principles, rules, and guidelines formulated or adopted by an organization to reach its long-term goals and typically published in a booklet or other form that is widely accessible.

Policies and procedures are designed to influence and determine all major decisions and actions, and all activities take place within the boundaries set by them.

Procedures are the specific methods employed to express policies in action in day-to-day operations of the organization.

Together, policies and procedures ensure that a point of view held by the governing body of an organization is translated into steps that result in an outcome compatible with that view.

4.1(c) *IMPLEMENTATION PHASE*

Strategy Implementation

Strategy implementation is the sum total of the activities and choices required for the execution of a strategic plan.

It is the process by which strategies and policies are put into action through the development of programs, budgets, and procedures.

(a) *Programs*

The purpose of a program is to make the strategy action oriented.

(b) *Budgets*

After programs have been developed, the budget process begins. Planning a budget is the last real check of a corporation has on feasibility of its selected strategy. An ideal strategy might be found to be completely impractical only after specific implementation programs are costed.

(c) *Procedures*

After programs and budgets are approved, procedures must be developed.

Standard Operation Procedures (SOPs), they typically describe the various activities that must be carried out to complete a corporate program.

The procedures ensures that the day to day operations will be consistent over time and location.

4.1(d) *MONITORING PHASE*

Evaluation and Control

It ensures that the company is achieving what is set out to accomplish. It compares performance with desired results and provides feedback necessary for management, to evaluate results and take corrective actions as needed.

Performance

Performance is the end result of the activity which measures to select the assessed performance depends on the organization unit to be appraised and the objective to be achieved.

4.2 VISION

4.2(a) *MEANING*

Vision statement is company's road map, indicating both what the company wants to become and guiding transformational initiatives by setting a defined direction for the company's growth.

An aspirational description of what an organization would like to achieve (or) accomplish in the mid-term (or) long-term future. It is intended to serve as a clear guide for choosing current and future courses of action.

4.2(b) *ELEMENTS OF AN EFFECTIVE VISION STATEMENT*

The vision statement, a key elements of a strategic plan, needs to incorporate many elements:

1. **Audacious.** Vision represents a dream that's beyond the company's need and objective. It represents the mountain top the company is striving to reach. Visioning takes you out beyond the present reality.

2. **Capitalizes on Core Competencies.** Vision build on the company's core competencies. It builds on what the company already established, viz.

- Company history
- Customer Base
- Strength
- Unique Capabilities
- Resources
- Assets.

3. **Future Casting.** Vision provides a picture of what the company looks like in the future.

4. Inspiring. Vision engages language that inspires. It creates a vivid image on employee's emotions and excitement. It creates enthusiasm and poses a challenge among the employees.

5. Motivating. Vision clarifies the direction in which your organization needs to move and keep everyone pushing forward to reach it.

6. Purpose Driven. Vision gives a large sense of purpose, which enable the employees to accomplish the objectives.

4.2(c) *CHARACTERISTICS OF A VISION STATEMENT*

Although most leaders craft a vision statement for their organizations, many vision statements are not as powerful and as clear as they should be.

A powerful vision statement is the differentiator between organizations that achieve great results no matter what adversities they may face and those that disappear once they hit the first storm. A true vision statement links you with your passion which provides you and your people energy and moves you forward toward fulfilling your dreams and leaving a legacy behind.

1. Vision Statement should be Positive

Positive words generate positive energy. Positive statement are filled with positive energy. Vision declaration should include positive words in order to radiate positive energy so that when people read it or hear it they feel connected.

Replace negative words with positive ones and low impact words with high impact ones.

For instance if your vision is "As a team we never fail!", you may revise it to "As a team we always win!" to make it positive. You may even change it to "As a team we always thrive by moving forward!" to make it even more positive and impactful.

2. Vision Statement should be in Present Tense

Vision refers to visualizing the future and painting it at present. It is like living the dream. Vision statement in future tense, is far from reach or something that would happen sometime in future. It might not connect much to vision announcements in future tense.

However, the vision statement in present tense, it feels like that we are living it. It becomes alive. As a result our subconscious mind conditions itself for believing and achieving it.

Now, review your vision testimony and change the verbs to present tense, if any. For instance, "As a team we will win!" can be replaced by "As a team we always win!" The impact of the latter statement is much more than the first one.

3. Vision Statement should be Short

Lengthy vision descriptions typically lose their impact and may cause people to disconnect. Short and clear yet rich and powerful vision statements are easy to remember and easy to communicate.

As an example, this long sentence "We help big corporate companies, organizations, small companies, communities, teams, families, couples, and individuals build upon their strengths, transform their weaknesses to strengths, and as a result grow and succeed" can be replaced by "We help our customers grow and succeed".

4. Vision Statement should be Challenging

Powerful vision testimonies pose some challenges to motivate people for growth and achieving something bigger. A visionary leader dreams something big enough to challenge themselves and their organizations and take everyone out of their comfort zones. When there is no challenge, there is no growth.

For instance, the statement "We provide solutions to our customers" may be an ordinary sentence. However, "We are the global leader in providing creative solutions to our customers" is definitely more challenging as it demands for becoming the global lead in providing creative solutions.

5. Vision Statement should be Relating

If people cannot relate themselves to the vision, it is like not having vision at all. Vision descriptions should touch people in one way or another. When people can relate themselves to the vision, they become interested in fulfilling the vision.

Vision statements should also relate to the organization's core values and mission. Those visions that have roots in core values will keep you and your organization on track during turbulent times as long as you stick to your core values.

4.3 MISSION

The mission describes the organization values, aspirations and reasons for being. It reveals the long-term vision of an organization in terms of what it wants to be, where exactly it wants to go and to whom it wants to serve.

The mission reflects the purpose of the organization, concerning particularly why it is in existence, nature of business it is in and the customers it seeks to serve and satisfy.

4.3(a) *MEANING OF MISSION STATEMENT*

The mission is an enduring statement of purpose that distinguishes one business firm from other similar firms. It identifies the scope of its operation in product and market terms.

It implies the image of the firm and reflects the values and priorities of the firm's strategic decision maker.

4.3(b) *DEFINITION*

According to John Pearce-II, A mission as "An enduring statement of purpose that distinguishes one business from other similar firms. It identifies the scope of its operation in product and market terms."

4.3(c) *CHARACTERISTICS OF A MISSION STATEMENT*

1. Mission of the firm should be very clear, both in terms of intentions and words used.
2. It should be fairly feasible and conceivable. The expressions regarding purpose should not be too high and unachievable and it should not demotivate the people.

3. The mission should be precise, concise and fairly explanatory, neither too narrow, so to restrict the organization's activities, nor to broad too make itself meaningless.
4. It should be distinctive, both in terms of organization's contribution to the society and how these contribution can be made.
5. The statement of mission should be clearly articulated, The mission statement should be succinct and easy to understand so that the values and purpose, and goals of the organization are clear to everybody in the organization and will be guide to them.
6. A mission statement should be relevant and appropriate to the organization in the terms of history, culture and shared values.
7. At times mission statement may become stale and obsolete after sometime. Hence, care should be taken to make it current by suitably redefining according to the changing circumstances.
8. The mission statement should be positive tone and the tenor and the language should be inspiring.
9. The Mission statement should have an individuality of the firm, if not uniqueness.

4.3(d) *NEED FOR A MISSION STATEMENT*

Defining the mission of a business is entirely an integral agenda of accompany. No external agency can probably help in this regard, because it is the way a specific company would like to conduct its business to attain a certain desired objectives. It is a very painful, tedious and time-consuming exercise, but it is vital for any company or business. It contains a few specific areas of thrust, broadly carved out goals and strategies, and is a statement reflecting attitude, outlook, thinking-pattern, orientation and directly of the company.

We have discussed above the need for a mission statement. However, to summarize, we may state the following for evolving a mission statement.

(a) The mission statement gives a ***unified direction*** to the company's Growth.

(b) The ***Utilisation of Company's resources*** is also unified, and people get motivated to exploit these resources in a specific direction for the company's growth.

(c) ***Allocation of resources*** is based on the mission statement. Company executives get an idea for allocation of resources as directed by mission statement.

(d) The mission statement while giving a ***direction for growth*** also tends to build up a professional climate for maintenance and improvement of the company's status in any desired area. Thus it streamlines the functioning of the organization.

(e) The mission statement vividly brings forth the ***purpose and growth*** direction in the prevalent cultural climate of an organization, thus brings into focus the style of management of functioning of the organization. This approach draws support from people who wish to grow with the organization.

(f) The mission statement ***outlines a framework for organizational planning,*** assigning definite tasks and responsibilities of each business unit.

(g) The mission statement helps to ***set-up and develop a control mechanism*** or achievement of objectives.

(h) Defining the mission of an organization ***brings forth the hidden talent*** amongst the work force who take up challenges to meet the company's strategic objectives.

4.3(e) *COMPONENTS OF A MISSION STATEMENT*

There are nine components which the strategist think are essential in mission statement. Nine components presence in the mission statement is not mandatory but business mission statement with these nine ingredients consider as the best mission statement.

1. Customer. Mission statement should include answer the question, "Who are firm customers?"

2. Products and services. What are the firms major products and services?

3. Markets. Define the markets in which the firm competing?

4. Technology. Define the technology which the firm using for running their business.

5. Concern of survival, growth and profitability. Is the firm committed to growth and financial soundness.

6. Philosophy. The basic, belief, values, aspirations, and ethical priorities of the firm.

7. Self concept. The firm's distinctive competence or major competitive advantage.

8. Concern of public image. Is the firm responsive to social, community, and environmental concerns?

9. Concern of employees. Are employees valuable asset of the firm?

4.4 BUSINESS DEFINITION

4.4(a) *MEANING*

Business definition is a clear cut statement of the business or set of businesses, the organization engages in presently or wishes to pursue in future.

This prescribes the arena in which the organization will play and compete. It is a pre-requisite for future course of action.

4.4(b) *ASPECTS OF BUSINESS DEFINITION*

1. Focus in Business Definition. While defining a business, an organization should focus on its chosen field of business activity.

Focus of business may be defined in terms of the kind of functions of business performs rather than the broad spectrum of industry in which the organization operates.

Example: TEXTILE INDUSTRY

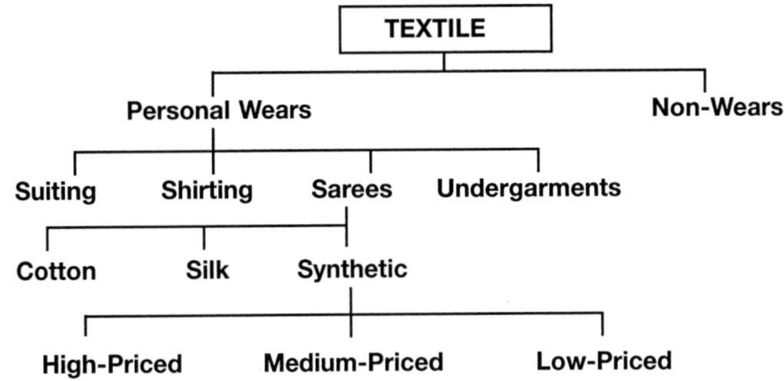

The company actually operates high-priced, premium synthetic sarees.

Sharp focus on business definition provides direction to a company to take suitable actions including positioning of the company's business.

2. Differentiation in Business Definition. Another feature involved in defining business is differentiation (i.e.) How does an organization differentiate itself from others? So, that the business concentrates on achieving superior performance in the market. Differentiation can be developed on several bases

- Quality
- Price
- Delivery
- Services
- Other factors

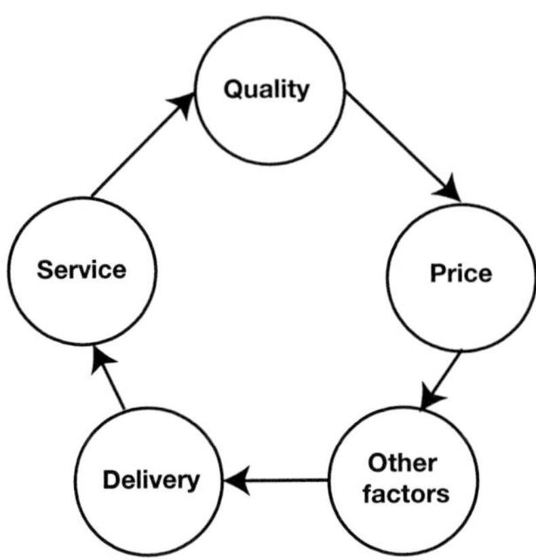

The company can differentiate from others according to their strength and opportunities available for them.

For Example:

A organization cannot differentiate on both quality and price at the same time because both move in the same direction, it cannot keep its product quality high at low cost.

4.5 GOALS AND OBJECTIVES

Objectives and goals are the end result which an organization strives for. Objectives and goals that are being pursued presently are for future of the company, and hence must be carefully defined.

Companies set their objectives and translate them into short- and long-term goals. An effort is usually made to set measurable goals such that performance of company can be objectively worked out. Any company doing business has a will to secure its survival through continuous growth and profitability.

> Desired states or outcomes are objectives. Goals are objectives that are scheduled for attainment during planned period.
>
> Goals are long-term aims the organization wants to accomplish.
>
> Objectives are concrete attainments that can be achieved by following a certain number of steps.
>
> Goals and objectives are often used interchangeably, but the main difference comes in their level of concreteness. Objectives are very concrete, whereas goals are less structured.

Objectives and goals in an organization provide the foundation for all the managerial activities. They can be considered as ends or aims towards which all activities are directed.

According to Brown and Moberg, objectives and goals serve the following function in an organization:

1. Aid in legitimating the organization.
2. Assist in identifying inter-organizational relationships.
3. Aid in building a public relations value.
4. Help attract support from different agencies and also attract right people to the organization.
5. Facilitate image buliding with the different players in the business environment, like suppliers, customers, policy makers and government.
6. Make coordination of the multiple task easier.
7. Help in resolving conflicts.

Goals

Goals are long-term aims the organization wants to accomplish.

Goal is an open-ended statement of what an organization wants to accomplish without qualification and time criteria. Goals can be considered as motivators in an organization. They can pose a challenge to its members and generate commitment from them.

An organization has to translate its purpose into long-term objectives and short-term goals for realizing its mission.

4.5(a) *CLASSIFICATION OF GOALS*

Goals can be classified into three types:

- Official goals
- Operative goals
- Operational goals

Official Goals serve the purpose of public relations value and help in legitimising the organization in the business environment.

Operative Goals provide an indication of what an organization is really attempting to do. Generally, these can be inferred from the actual operating policy. They can help focus attention, reduce uncertainity, and provide a choice of organizational design alternatives to choose from.

Operational Goals refer to those used by supervisory personnel to supervise the performance of subordinates and thereby influence their behaviour.

4.6 OBJECTIVES

Objectives are the end-result of planned activity. It states what is to be accomplished by when and should be quantified if possible. The achievement of the corporate objectives should result in the fulfillment of a corporation's mission.

Objectives can be defined as "the long-term result that an organization seeks to achieve in pursuing its basic mission".

Objectives should not be static, they should be Dynamic, i.e., changes in the environment or changes in the organizational strengths and weakness may call for modification of objectives. Objectives are operational definitions of the organizational goals. They provide measurable parameters for evaluating the performance of the organization.

4.6(a) *IMPORTANCE OF OBJECTIVES*

1. Objectives indicates the purpose and aims and thereby the social justification for the existence of an organization.
2. It provides directions for the functioning of an organization.
3. It helps an organization to adjust itself to the existing environment.
4. It helps in attaining employees coordination and thereby reduces conflicts.
5. It provides the basis for control and assessment of organization performance.
6. It helps Decentralization by assigning decision-making to lower level personnel.

4.6(b) *ROLE OF OBJECTIVES*

The objectives of the organization plays a vital role in creating environment for growth in desired direction. The role of the objectives are as follows:

1. The objectives establish a relationship between an organization and the environment in which it exists. The environment consists of various entities like society, politics, customers, stakeholders.
2. Objectives are the driving force of an organization. The employees make a unified effort to accomplish them, thereby developing a clarity of mission and purpose.
3. Strategic decision-making process become sharply focussed due to objectives, and a code of behaviour is also set for meeting the targets. The strategic decisions are taken around agreed objectives.
4. Objectives leads to evolution of standards for performance evaluation and measures to control and guide performance. Standards for individual performance are also generated since it is the individual performance that eventually gets translated to organizational performance.
5. Objectives tend to develop conductive environment, understanding of business environment, organization, personal development, required knowledge, skills and attitude.

4.6(c) *CHARACTERISTICS OF OBJECTIVES*

1. Objectives should be Understandable. Objectives play an important role in strategic management and are put to use in various ways, they should be understandable by those who have to achieve them. A chief executive who says that, "something ought to be done to set things right" or not likely to be understood by his managers.

2. Objectives should not be Concrete and Specific. Objectives of an organization should be specific and concrete, it should not be subject to changes. A clear cut idea must be ensured among the employees so as to accomplish those objectives.

3. Objectives should be Related to a Time Frame. Objectives must essentially be related to time dimension. The business situations today undergo extremely fast changes, and not relating objectives to a time-dimension may prove to be very costly for companies. Objectives when related to time, communicate more specific information. Objectives without time frame do not yield much results.

4. Objectives should be Measurable and Controllable. It should be possible to measure and control the factors which define objectives. This leads to development of a mechanism in a company, by way of which various parameters are measured and controlled in order to accomplish objectives.

5. Objectives should be challenging. Objectives should be optimally stretched in such a way that they pose a challenge to the workforce and motivate them to work better. This leads to improved performance of a company, and strategy managers can take up the challenge for achieving an improved status for their company. It is necessary that the stretched goals be set in agreement with employees of a company. This develops a sense of belonging in the minds of the employees of a company.

6. Objective should Correlate with each other. Objective should correlate with each other in order to avoid the conflicts within two related departments. An objective should offer synergic advantage, and should strike an optimum balance between the variables.

7. Objectives should be Set within the Constrains. Objectives must be set keeping the practical constraint in view. The strategy managers must be well aware of the internal and external constraints. The internal constraints could be availability of raw materials, trained and skilled personnel etc. The external constraints may be legal and statutory requirements, norms of pollution and effluents and companies have to keep these constraints in mind before arriving the final objectives.

4.6(d) *DIFFERENCES BETWEEN OBJECTIVES AND GOALS*

1. Time Frame

Objectives are timeless, enduring, and unending.

Goals are temporal, time-phased, and intended to be superceded by subsequent goals.

2. Specificity

Objectives are stated in broad, general terms, dealing with mattes of image, style and self-perception. These are aspirations to be worked in future.

Goals are much more specific, stated in terms of a particular result that will be accomplished by a specific period.

3. Focus

Objectives are usually stated in terms of some relevant environment which is external to the organization.

Goals are more internally focused and carry important implications about how the organization are utilized or will how utilized in future.

4. Measurement

Both objectives and goals can be stated in terms which are quantitatively measured but the character of measurement is different.

Chapter 5

Environmental Scanning

An organization has to scan the external environment to identify possible opportunities and threats and the internal environment for its strengths and weaknesses before it can start on strategy formulation. The monitoring, evaluation and dissemination of information from the external and internal environment to key personnel within the organization constitutes environmental scanning, which is used to avoid strategic surprise and ensures long-term health of the organization. There is a positive relationship between environmental scanning and profits as borne out by research.

According to Kotler, "Environmental threats a challenge posed by an unfavorable trend or development. Environmental opportunity for a company is an attractive area in which the company would enjoy a competitive advantage".

5.1 ASPECTS OF ENVIRONMENTAL SCANNING

1. Monitoring the environment, i.e. environment search.
2. Identifying opportunities and threats based on environment monitoring, i.e. environment diagnosis.
3. Identifying strengths and weakness of an organization.

5.2 FEATURES OF ENVIRONMENTAL ANALYSIS

1. Holistic Exercise

Environment Analysis is a holistic exercise in which total view of environment is taken rather than viewing trends in piece meal.

Here, the environment is divided into different components to find out their nature, and relationship for searching opportunities and threats and determining where they come from ultimately the analysis of these components is aggregated to have the total view of environment.

Some elements may indicate opportunities and others indicate threats.

2. Heuristic/Exploratory Process

While monitoring aspects of the environment is concerned with present developments, a large part of the process seeks to explore the unknown terrain, the dimensions of possible futures.

The future is uncertain and the analysis must be an alternative futures, seeking classification of the assumptions about the flow. Speculating about the flow, speculating systematically about alternative customers.

3. Continuous Process

Environment analysis must be a continuous process rather than becoming an intermittent scanning system.

Continuous scanning of environment ensures the picking up of new signals or triggers in the overall pattern of developing trends.

5.3 ROLE OF ENVIRONMENTAL ANALYSIS

Role of environmental analysis in strategic management is quite crucial.

Ian Wilson has compared the role of environmental analysis with function of radar. If a ship is sailing on a sea of uncertainty, there are two essential requirements for a successful voyage. There has to be a star to steer the ship. Secondly, there must be radar to signal the existence of rock, reefs, and clear water in the uncharted sea. Similarly, a business firm operating in an uncertain environment, must have a vision of the business (a guiding star) and system of environmental analysis (the radar).

Many of the research studies also suggest that those organizations which undertake systematic environmental analysis perform better than those which do not take such an exercise. For example, Danny and Friesen's research study shows high relationship between environmental analysis and success of the firms. Even in our country, Reliance Industries Limited gives very high priority to environmental analysis and the result is that the company has achieved highest growth rate in Indian corporate sector. The role of environmental analysis in strategic management can be seen in the following ways:

1. The environment changes so fast that new opportunities and threats are created which may result into disequilibrium into organization's existing equilibrium. Therefore, the strategists have to analyze the environment to determine what factors in the environment present opportunities for greater accomplishment of organizational objectives and what factors in the environment present threats to the organization's objective accomplishment so that suitable adjustment in strategies can be made to derive maximum benefits.
2. Environmental analysis allows strategists time to anticipate opportunities and plan to take optional responses to these opportunities. Similarly, it helps to develop an early warning system to prevent the threats or to develop strategies which can turn the threats to the organization's advantage.
3. Environmental analysis helps strategists to narrow the range of available alternatives and eliminate options that are clearly inconsistent with forecast opportunities or threats. The analysis helps in eliminating unsuitable alternatives and to process most promising alternatives. Thus, it helps strategists to reduce time pressure and to concentrate on those which are more important.

5.4 FACTORS TO BE CONSIDERED FOR ENVIRONMENTAL SCANNING

Given the same environmental conditions, no two strategists or two organizations would appraise the environment in a similar fashion. This is due to the many factors that affect the process of environmental appraisal. We could identify these factors by classifying them into three categories: the strategist-related, organization-related and environment-related factors.

1. Strategist-related Factors

There are many factors related to the strategist, which affect the process of environmental appraisal. Since strategists play a central role in the formulation of strategies, their characteristics such as age, education, experience, motivation level, cognitive styles, ability to withstand the time pressures and strain, etc. have an impact on the extent to which they are able to appraise their organization's environment and how well they are able to do it. Apart from these factors, related to strategists as individuals, group characteristics too have an impact on how well-environmental appraisal is done. Such group characteristics could be the interpersonal relations between the different strategists involved in appraisal, team spirit, and the power equations operating between them.

2. Organization-related Factors

Like those of strategists, many characteristics of the organization also have an impact on the environmental appraisal process. These characteristics are the nature of business the organization is in, its age, size and complexity, the nature of its markets, and the product or services that it provides.

3. Environment-related Factors

The nature of environment facing an organization determines how its appraisal could be done. The nature of the environment depends on its complexity, volatility or turbulence, hostility, and diversity.

In sum, how well-environmental appraisal is done depends on the strategists, their organizations, and the environment in which their organizations exist.

Before strategists can structure the environmental appraisal, it is necessary to identify the environmental factors.

5.5 APPROACHES TO ENVIRONMENTAL SCANNING

Kuber has suggested three approaches which could be adopted for sorting out information for environmental scanning. We could call these approaches as systematic, ad hoc and processed-form approaches.

1. Systematic Approach

Under this approach, information for environmental scanning is collected systematically. Information related to markets and customers, changes in legislation and regulations that have a direct impact on an organization's business and industry, etc. could be collected continuously to monitor changes and take the relevant factors into account. Continuously updating such information is necessary not only for strategic management but also for operational activities.

2. Ad hoc Approach

Using this approach, an organization may conduct special surveys and studies to deal with specific environmental issues from time to time. Such studies may be conducted, for instance, when an organization has to undertake special projects, evaluate existing strategies or devise new strategies. Changes and unforeseen developments may also be investigated with regard to their impact on the organization.

3. Processed-form Approach

For adopting this approach, the organization uses information in a processed form available from different sources both inside and outside the organization. When an organization uses information supplied by government agencies or private institutions, it uses secondary sources of data and the information is available in a processed form.

Since environmental scanning is absolutely necessary for strategy formulation, organizations use different practical combinations of approaches to monitor their relevant environments. These approaches may range from an informal assessment of environmental factors to a highly systematic and formal procedure. Informal assessment may be adopted as a reactive measure to a crisis and ad hoc studies may be undertaken occasionally. A highly systematic and formal procedure may be used as a proactive measure in anticipation of changes in environmental factors and structured data collected and processing systems may be used continuously. Between the two extremes of the informal and formal approaches may lie different stances adopted by organizations depending on varying degrees of concern. Such stances are situational. For example, when an issue-related decision has to be taken, periodic monitoring of the environment may be done. Systematic and ad hoc approaches can be used for the relevant environment of the organization while the processed-form approach could be used to appraise both the relevant as well as the general environment. Whatever approach is adopted for environmental scanning, data collection is necessary for deriving information about environmental factors.

5.6 SOURCES OF INFORMATION FOR ENVIRONMENTAL SCANNING

The various sources of information tapped for collecting data for environmental scanning could be classified in different ways. There could be formal and informal sources. Then there could be written as well as verbal sources. In terms of origin, data sources could be external and internal.

Given below are some of the important types of sources of information.

1. Documentary or secondary sources of information like different types of publications. These could be newspapers, magazines, journals, books, trade and industry association newsletters, government publications, annual reports of competitor companies, etc.
2. Mass media such as radio and television.
3. Internal sources like company files and documents, management information system, company employees, etc.
4. External agencies like customers, marketing intermediaries, suppliers, trade associations, government agencies, etc.
5. Formal studies done by employees, market research agencies, consultants and educational institutions.
6. Spying and surveillance through ex-employees of competitors, industrial espionage agencies, or by planting 'moles' in competitor companies.

Strategists use different information sources depending on their needs for environmental scanning. Government publications, though they are rich and comprehensive source of information, usually are available after a considerable time lag. Private sources, though relevant and timely, are quite expensive to tap.

5.7 TAXONOMY OF FIRMS ENVIRONMENT

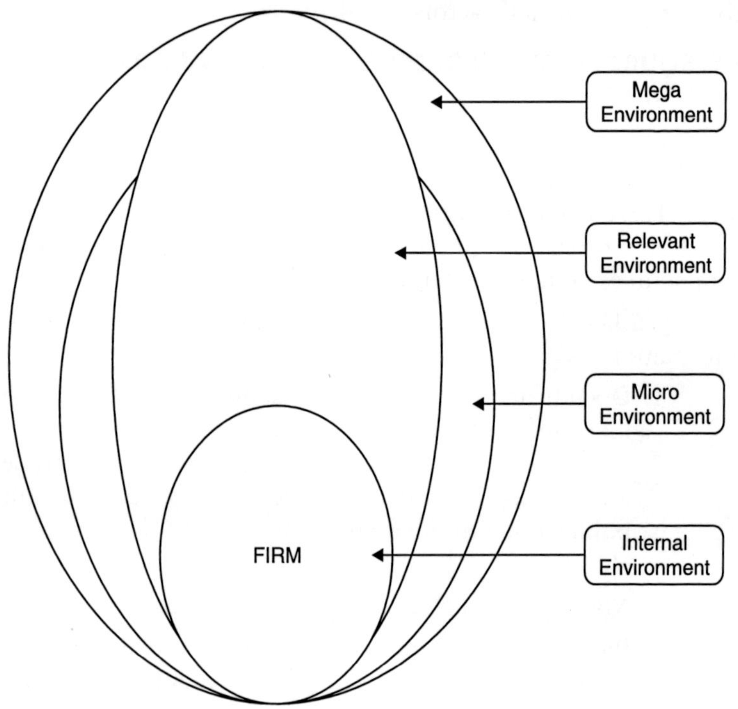

We look at an organization under three heads:

1. Mega environment
2. Micro environment
3. Relevant environment

From the figure, it can be seen that the mega environment skirts the micro and the relevant environments.

The micro environment has a substantial impact on the organization's current business. Developments in micro-environment will affect strategic decisions of the organization. Typically, its constituents are competitors, suppliers, customers, financial institutions, regulatory organizations, channels of distribution, etc.

The relevant environment refers to the primary business focus of the organization. In essence, the relevant environment encompasses some of the elements from the micro and the mega environments, which is of interest to the organization. It should be noted that it is impossible to take advantage of all the opportunities that may be present in micro and mega environment by an organization.

The relevant environment has to be considered along with the internal environment of the organization, i.e. the strengths and weaknesses of the organization to analyse the impact of the opportunities and threats in the environment. An organization has to restrict its scope and search for business opportunities and also safeguard itself against threats that may be present.

Changes in environment are frequent and often unpredictable. It is incumbent on an organization to keep pace with these changes.

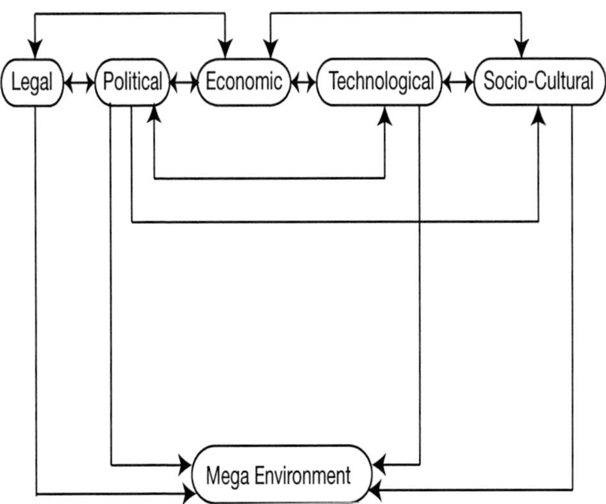

I *MEGA ENVIRONMENT*

The important constituents of the mega environment are economic, technological, political, legal and socio-cultural factors. The mega environment is also referred to as societal environment.

I(a) *Technological Environment*

The impact of technological developments on strategy is not only fast but is far reaching. It can expand or reduce the opportunities for an organization. It has to be recognized that the pace of technological developments has increased. The growth of the information technology sector has acted as a catalyst in this direction. The future will witness the pace of technology developments becoming much faster.

The Government of India has laid emphasis on technological advances by setting up "technology missions". These are intended for the following:

- Providing drinking water
- Promoting literacy
- Stepping up child immunization
- Increasing production of oilseeds
- Linking remote areas with the country's telecommunication network.

Corporate response to technological advances should be entrepreneurial and not reactive. It calls for a changed outlook and ability to take risks. Failure to modernize and change the product mix according to market needs may have serious implications for the survival of the organization. This is in fact the reason for the decline and sickness of the textile industry.

It becomes imperative that certain technological consideration be included in the environmental analysis for strategic decision-making. These can be:

- Future form of product group
- Future processing technology
- Future form of raw materials
- Technological developments in unrelated areas

- Stages of technological development in terms of invention, innovation and diffusion.

I(b) *Socio-cultural Environment*

Socio-cultural changes occur gradually unlike technological changes. It is not easy to predict the timing of these changes. Areas where socio-cultural changes may have strong implications for organization are:

- Changes in lifestyle
- Pace of urbanization and its impact on family and societal values
- Spread of literacy
- Rate of family formation and growth of population
- Age distribution
- Health and life expectancy
- Expectations from business and social values
- Ethical standards.

Religious beliefs, attitudes towards foreigners, public opinion on human rights and environmentalism are also important variables in socio-cultural environment scanning.

It is imperative that organizations modify or change their goals as society demands, since they exist in it. There is a trend towards improvement of business ethics in India, especially in the software industry. Improvements in ethical standards contribute not only to the health of the organization but also to the image of the country.

I(c) *Economic Environment*

For any strategic decision, a continuous monitoring of the economic environment is necessary. Economic indicators like GDP and its growth rate, proposed plan outlays, capital-output ratios, balance of trade, money supply, wholesale price index, retail price index, interest rates, per capita income and its growth rate have to be monitored closely to get a fair idea of the economy's health. Some of the organizations that publish this information are Centre for Monitoring of the Indian Economy (CMIE), Reserve Bank of India (RBI), and

National Centre for Applied Economic Research (NCAER). Several magazines like Business India, Business Today and Indiatimes.com are also sources of information. With the ongoing process of liberalization, the areas reserved for the State is shrinking. There is greater flexibility for business houses.

I(d) *Political and Legal Environment*

It is possible that some of the indicators listed under "political and legal" may overlap with the economic environment. However, this should not in any way become a hindrance to decipher the total impact of a trend. Some of the important variables that constitute this environment are tax laws, stability of governance, attitude towards foreign companies, special incentives, and environment protection laws.

Some Important Variables in Mega Environment

Economic	Technological	Political & legal	Socio-cultural
GDP trends Interest rates	Spending by by government for R & D	Anti-trust Litigation	Lifestyle changes
Money supply Inflation rates	Total industry Spending for R & D	Environment protection laws	Career expectations
Unemployment rates Wage/ price controls	Focus of technology in Patent protection	Special incentives	Growth rate of population
Energy availability & Cost	New products	Foreign trade regulations	Age distribution of population
Devaluation/ revaluation	Commercialization & Transfer from lab to Market place	Attitudes towards foreign companies recruitment laws	Regional shifts in population
Disposable Discretionary income	Productivity improvements	Stability of government	Life expectancies birth rates.

Organizations should also focus on the form of government, its attitude towards foreign companies, foreign policy, terrorist activity, strength of opposition groups, and protectionist sentiment while analyzing the political and legal environment.

II *THE MICRO ENVIRONMENT*

II(a) *Suppliers*

'Suppliers' refer to suppliers of raw-material components, parts, expert services, etc., In other words, these are suppliers of basic inputs which help in the production of goods and services. Dependence on only one source of supply can pose threats to continuous production. In such a situation, the supplying firm will have a strategic advantage. In case the production firm is very strong, it can use its purchasing muscle to prevent its competitors from receiving supplies regularly. Thus, the firm's management of the flow of inputs determines the areas of threats and opportunities.

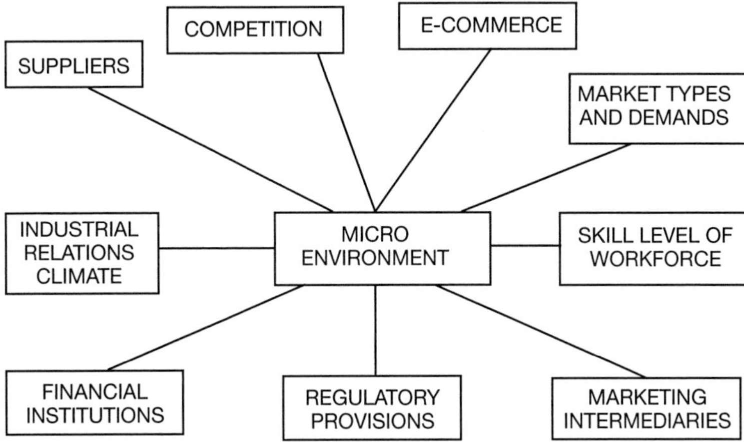

II(b) *Marketing Intermediaries*

The marketing intermediaries are the distribution channels. They can include services, advertising, transport and market research. In our country, up to the late 70s firms providing such professional services were not available. Over the years this situation has changed with the entry of firms specializing in providing such services. Marketing intermediaries perform the activities of search, distribution, communication, negotiation and title transfer.

Two types of marketing intermediaries are possible. They are:

- Agent middlemen
- Merchant middlemen

Though both agent middlemen and merchant middlemen perform the same marketing intermediary function, the merchant middlemen also takes title to transfer.

With the foray of the Internet into the markets, the working of the marketing intermediaries has changed. E-commerce has made it possible to establish a direct link with both the supplier and the end-user. To that extent the role of the marketing intermediaries has shrunk.

II(c) ***Market Types and Demands***

The various types of markets can be classified as:

- Consumer markets
- Industrial markets
- Institutional markets
- Organizational customers buying goods and services-either for their own use or for transfer
- International markets
- Foreign buyers who may include producers, resellers, etc.
- Others.

Market demand refers to the quantum, i.e. the sum total (both monetary and no. of units) that should be purchased in a given time period, behavior, i.e. seasonality-cyclic and trends in demand, production and structure, i.e. the kind of market the firm has. Seasonal and cyclic situations can make firms vulnerable during lean periods, for example, fertilizers, fans, etc.

From an Indian firm's point of view, to draw up a corporate strategy, the following additional issues also need to be addressed:

Market behavior for developing and poor economies are largely unpredictable. Hence, in spite of the liberalization process, the market size available to Indian firms is not very big. This prevents them from seeking the benefits of economies of scale. Therefore, it is very important for an Indian firm to look at the size of the market before entering it.

The financial institutions which have to be considered in our country are Industrial Development Bank of India (IDBI), Industrial Credit and Investment Corporation of India (ICICI), and leading commercial banks like the State Bank of India (SBI). With the onset of liberalization process, several private banks have entered the fray. Merger of HDFC and Bank of Madura and the formation of the UTI Bank are examples in this direction.

II(d) ***Industrial Climate***

The regulatory environment varies from industry to industry and location to location. Special incentives offer attractive opportunities to set up industries in particular areas. Some of these incentives could be abolition of sales tax, octroi, and tax rebate.

A disturbed industrial climate cannot be beneficial to an organization. Examples can be cited of disturbed industrial relations prevalent in the states of West Bengal and Kerala, where entrepreneurs are wary of setting up their enterprises due to labour problems. Peaceful industrial climate can be a major opportunity.

II(e) ***Regulatory Environment***

Regulatory environment is just opposite to promoting environment; it puts certain restrictions on the operations of business organizations. However, these restrictions are not of arbitrary nature but are based on the nature a social system. In Indian context, regulatory environment consists of the factors related to the regulation of business operations of business and practices that they are required to follow in conducting their business. These have been prescribed by legislative measures in the form of various laws and policy formulation from time to time. Though many changes have taken place in India's regulatory environment.

1. Control through industrial policies and licensing,
2. Control of monopolies and restrictive trade practices,
3. Control through Foreign Exchange Management Act,
4. Control on import and export,

5. Control over foreign operations, collaboration and joint venture,
6. Control over distribution and pricing of certain goods,
7. Control to protect consumer interest,
8. Control over environmental pollution, and
9. Control of procedural matters through the competitors Act.

5.8 TECHNIQUES OF ENVIRONMENTAL SCANNING

Various techniques available for environmental scanning are:

- SWOT
- PEST
- QUEST
- Industrial Analysis
- Competitor Analysis

5.8(a) *SWOT ANALYSIS*

Relating Opportunities and Resources (Situation Analysis—Opportunities and Threats Analysis)

Strategic management is concerned with establishing the proper organization. It creates environment fit for matching organizational factors with the environmental factors. Therefore, strategic management involves an analysis of the organizational strengths and weakness and the environmental opportunities and threats. Strategists must clearly ascertain strategic fit between external opportunities and internal strengths while working around external threats and internal weakness. This process is called situation analysis.

An opportunity by itself has little value to an organization unless it has the capacity to extract that opportunity. Organization must be in a position to deploy its resources carefully and in a most profitable manner. Organization must use its core competencies and resources to secure competitive advantage. Core competences lead to the development of core products to attract more and more customers.

Situation analysis is also popularly known as SWOT analysis—strength, weakness, opportunities and threats.

SWOT analysis helps an organization to match its strengths and weaknesses with opportunities and threats operating in the environment. An appropriate strategy is one that capitalizes on the opportunities by using organizational resources and capabilities to the best advantage an neutralizes the threats by minimizing the adverse influence of weaknesses.

Strengths

Strengths are the internal capabilities of an organization which can be used to gain competitive advantage over its competitors. It also includes ability of the organization to perform certain activities better than its competitor. Following factors contributes strength of the organization:

- Physical assets, like building, plant and machinery, financial resources, strategic location of the plant/raw material, distribution networks etc.
- Human assets like intellectual capital, talented R&D people etc.
- Good accounting policies, strategic planning system and HR practices.
- High quality manufacturing, brand image, committed and talented sales force.
- Licenses and patent rights exclusively held by the company.

Weakness

Limitations or constraints which tend to decrease the competencies of the organization particularly in comparison to its competitors. Weakness may exist due to non-availability of a particular resource with the organization. This may arise due to any of the following reasons:

- Lack of physical, human, organizational assets that are critical to the survival of the organization.
- Lack of appropriate skill in utilizing resources.
- Lack of strategic direction for the company.

Opportunities

Major favourable conditions (care competencies) in the organization which help an organization strengthen its position. Opportunities are those favourable situations the company is equipped to capture. The opportunities that may arise are:

- Emergence of new customer segments in the market.
- Changes in customers buying habits and potentials.
- Changes in technological, social, legal and economic environment.
- Evaluation of opportunities should be limited to only those opportunities that the organization can utilize with its existing resources.

Threats

Major unfavourable conditions in the organization which may pose a risk or damage the firm's position in comparison to its competitors. An organization threats are those factors in a company environment that the firm is not equipped to handle. Environment threat may arise due to the following changes:

- Entry of new competitors with better business models.
- Change in technology for which organization is not affordable.
- Change in customer habit for which organization is not in a position to respond quickly, which may shift their customers to their competitors.

Use of SWOT Analysis

SWOT (acronym for the internal strengths and weaknesses of a firm and the environment opportunities and threats facing that firm) analysis helps an organization match its strengths and weaknesses with opportunities and threats operating in the environment. An appropriate strategy is one that capitalizes on the opportunities by using organizational resources and capabilities to the best advantage and neutralizes the threats by minimizing the adverse influence of weaknesses.

Strengths: Internal capabilities of a firm which can be used to gain competitive advantage over its rivals.

- **Weaknesses:** Limitations or constrains which tend to decrease the competencies of the firm particularly in comparison to its rivals.
- **Opportunities:** Major favourable conditions in a firm's environment which help a firm strengthen its position.
- **Threats:** Major unfavourable conditions in a firm's environment which may pose a risk or damage the firm's position in comparison to its rivals.

"SWOT" Matrix

The SWOT Matrix, developed by Heinz Welhrich, is an important strategy formulation-matching tool. The SWOT Matrix states the following four alternative strategies:

	Internal strengths (s)	Internal weakness (w)
External opportunities	SO (maxi-maxi) Strategy (maximize strengths & opportunities)	WO (mini-maxi) Strategy (minimize weakness and maximize opportunities)
External threats	ST (maxi-mini) Strategy (maximize strengths & minimize threats)	WT (mini-mini) Strategy (minimize weakness and threats)

1. **"WT" strategy/mini-mini strategy.** The "WT" or the mini-mini strategy seeks to **minimize the weaknesses and threats.** Some of the weaknesses may be overcome or minimized. For example, managerial weakness may be solved by change of managerial personnel, training, etc. Weakness due to excess manpower may be addressed to by restructuring and retirement schemes. External threat may be met by strategic alliance or other types of joint ventures. In some cases an unprofitable business that cannot be revived may be given up.

2. **"WO" strategy/mini-maxi strategy.** The "WO" or mini-maxi strategy aims at **minimizing the weaknesses and maximizing the opportunities.** For example, for a textile machinery manufacturer in India the main weaknesses were dependence on foreign firms for technology and the long-time taken to execute an order. The solutions are to give thrust to R&D to develop technology and measures to reduce the time lag so as to be in a better position to exploit to the maximum the growing demand.

3. "ST" Strategy/Maxi-mini strategy. The "ST" strategy or maxi-mini strategy **aims at maximizing strength and minimizing threat** attempts to use the organization's strengths to deal with the environmental threats. For example, a company may use its technological, financial and marketing strengths to combat a new competition. For example, Hindustan Lever has been employing this strategy to fight the increasing competition from companies like P&G, Nirma, etc.

4. "SO" Strategy/Maxi-maxi strategy. The "SO" or maxi-maxi strategy **aims at maximizing strength and maximizing opportunities** which is the most desirable and advantageous strategy, seeks to mass up a firm's strengths to exploit the opportunities. For instance, Hindustan Lever has been augmenting its strengths (by measures such as the merger of BBLIL into HLL and takeover of firms like Moden Food, Kissan in the food business) to exploit the growing potential of the food business.

Critical Success Factors (CSFs) Or Key Success Factors (KSFs)

While formulating organizational objectives, managers must concentrate on key factors which ensure organization success. CSFs allow the business organization to concentrate on a particular area and exploit the opportunities. If management allocates resources exactly the same way competitors do, there will be no change in competitive position.

Key success factor could arise from both industry environment and specific considerations.

5.8(b) *PEST ANALYSIS*

The important constituents of the mega environment are economic, technological, political, legal and socio-cultural factors. The mega environment is also referred to as societal environment.

Technological Environment

The impact of technological developments on strategy is not only fast but is far reaching. It can expand or reduce the opportunities for an organization. It has to be recognized that the pace of technological developments has increased. The growth of the information technology sector has acted as a catalyst in this direction. The future will witness the pace of technology developments becoming much faster.

The Government of India has laid emphasis on technological advances by setting up "technology missions". These are intended for the following:

- Providing drinking water
- Promoting literacy
- Stepping up child immunization
- Increasing production of oilseeds
- Linking remote areas with the country's telecommunication network.

Corporate response to technological advances should be entrepreneurial and not reactive. It calls for a changed outlook and ability to take risks. Failure to modernize and change the product mix according to market needs may have serious implications for the survival of the organization. This is in fact the reason for the decline and sickness of the textile industry.

It becomes imperative that certain technological consideration be included in the environmental analysis for strategic decision-making. These can be

- Future form of product group
- Future processing technology
- Future form of raw materials
- Technological developments in unrelated areas
- Stages of technological development in terms of invention, innovation and diffusion.

Socio-cultural Environment

Socio-cultural changes occur gradually unlike technological changes. It is not easy to predict the timing of these changes. Areas where socio-cultural changes may have strong implications for organization are

- Changes in lifestyle

- Pace of urbanization and its impact on family and societal values
- Spread of literacy
- Rate of family formation and growth of population
- Age distribution
- Health and life expectancy
- Expectations from business and social values
- Ethical standards.

Religious beliefs, attitudes towards foreigners, public opinion on human rights and environmentalism are also important variables in socio-cultural environment scanning.

It is imperative that organizations modify or change their goals as society demands, since they exist in it. There is a trend towards improvement of business ethics in India, especially in the software industry. Improvements in ethical standards contribute not only to the health of the organization but also to the image of the country.

Economic Environment

For any strategic decision, a continuous monitoring of the economic environment is necessary. Economic indicators like GDP and its growth rate, proposed plan outlays, capital-output ratios, balance of trade, money supply, wholesale price index, retail price index, interest rates, per capita income and its growth rate have to be monitored closely to get a fair idea of the economy's health. Some of the organizations that publish this information are Centre for Monitoring of the Indian Economy (CMIE), Reserve Bank of India (RBI), and National Centre for Applied Economic Research (NCAER). Several magazines like Business India, Business Today and Indiatimes.com are also sources of information. With the ongoing process of liberalization, the areas reserved for the State is shrinking. There is greater flexibility for business houses.

Political and Legal Environment

It is possible that some of the indicators listed under "political and legal" may overlap with the economic environment. However, this should not in any way become a hindrance to decipher the total impact of a trend. Some of the important variables that constitute this environment are tax laws, stability of governance, attitude towards foreign companies, special incentives, and environment protection laws.

Economic	Technological	Political & legal	Socio-cultural
GDP trends Interest rates	Spending by government for R&D	Anti trust Litigation	Lifestyle changes
Money supply Inflation rates	Total industry Spending for R&D	Environment protection laws	Career expectations
Unemployment rates Wage/price controls	Focus of technology Patent protection	Special incentives	Growth rate of population
Devaluation/ revaluation	New products	Foreign trade regulations	Age distribution of population
Energy availability & Cost	Commercialization & Transfer from lab to Market place	Attitudes towards foreign companies Recruitment laws	Regional shifts in population
Disposable Discretionary income	Productivity improvements	Stability of government	Life expectancies birth rates

Organizations should also focus on the form of government, its attitude towards foreign companies, foreign policy, terrorist activity, strength of opposition groups, and protectionist sentiment while analyzing the political and legal environment.

5.8(c) *QUEST ANALYSIS*

A new approach called QUEST (Quick Environmental Scanning Techniques) has been developed to provide broad and comprehension first approximation to environmental trends and events that are critical to strategic decision.

Definition

Quest may be defined as a future research process designed to permit executives and planners in an organization to share their views about trends and events in future environment that have critical implication for the organization strategies and policies.

It is a systematic, intensive and relatively inexpensive way to develop a shared understanding of high priority issues to focus management attention quickly on strategic areas for which more detailed planning analysis would be beneficial.

The basic assumption of QUEST technique is that each member of the top management team of a corporation already has a view of the changing dynamic environment.

In the aggregate, these assumption represent the organization's understanding of its environment.

Task of QUEST Process

1. Preparation. In this phase, a group of 12-15 executives is chosen for participation In an intensive one day exercise. A notebook is prepared containing information on the major environment trends and events in the industry. The information is drawn from readily available trade association, government and other standard sources. An off-premise facility is reserved for a one day retreat and the participants are asked to review the notebook prior the meeting.

2. Divergent Planning Session. The participants proceed through a carefully structured series of discussions, starting with definition, performance indicator, major constituencies' trends and events and probabilities. Wide range of speculation on important issues might affect the future of the firm. An attempt is made to scan the horizon broadly and comprehensively.

3. Scenario Development. Based upon the data gathered, the QUEST director, who may be an outside consultant, prepares a report summarizing the major issues and implications. The report also synthesizes three to five scenarios incorporating the major themes.

The report is distributed to the participants prior to a second half day meeting which is usually held in a corporate facility.

4. Strategic Options Identifications. The report is reviewed, strength and weakness of the firm are discussed and then the group identifies feasible strategic options to deal with the evolving external environment.

The last step is the rank ordering of strategic options and the formation of planning teams to further development of high priority strategies.

QUEST Process

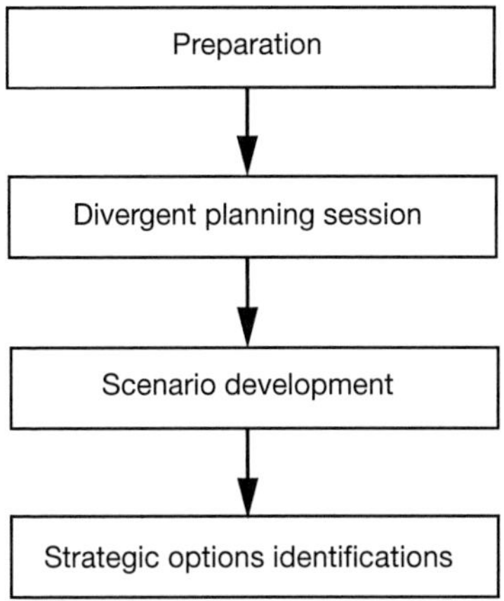

5.8(d) *INDUSTRIAL ANALYSIS*

Porter's Approach

An industry is defined as a group of organization that offers a similar product or class of products that are close substitute of each other. Industrial analysis can be undertaken by analyzing the following factors which determine the comprehensive nature of an industry:

1. Industry setting,
2. Industry structure,
3. Industry attractiveness,
4. Industry performance, and
5. Industry practices.

Industry Setting

Industry setting deals with the pattern or industries in terms of their stage of evolution and maturation as well as geographical dimension. On the basis of these, Porter has classified the various industries into five categories:

1. Fragmented Industries,
2. Emerging Industries,
3. Industries undergoing a transition to maturity,

4. Declining Industries, and
5. Global Industries.

1. **Fragmented Industry.** A fragmented industry is one which is scattered at numerous places with each place serving the local markets. There may be number of players in the industry. However, since the production technology is mostly non-mechanized, expansion of the industry beyond certain geographical area poses problems. Non-mechanised farm equipments, pottery, etc., fall in this category. Since industry players cater to a small area, their competitive advantage has narrow potential to reap large amount of benefits.

2. **Emerging Industry.** An emerging industry is one where market for product/s exists in latent form and it materializes later. In fact, most of the industries at one point of time, have been emerging ones.

For example, computer industry, at one point of time, was emerging industry in the form of various means of calculation such as abacuses, slide rules, and large adding machines.

Necessities of all these have led to the emergence of computers for faster manipulation of data. In emerging industry, buyer preferences scatter evenly and a company may have three options to design a product for differentiation and competitive advantage. First, the new product can be designed to meet the preferences of one part of the market. Second, two or more products can be launched simultaneously for two or more parts of the market. Third, the new product can be designed for the middle of the market.

3. **Industries Undergoing a Transition to Maturity.** Growth occurs in an industry over the period of time which ultimately leads to its maturity. When growth occurs in the industry, it attracts many competitors and, eventually, they cover the entire market segments. In fact, they go further and invade others' segments. Since growth rate of the industry does not match the growth rate of competitors, they focus on cutting the market shares of each other through various tools of differentiation and competitive advantages. For example, in India, growth rate of oral care product is much lower than the size of expansion

of different competitors. With the result, each competitor has concentrated on cutting the market shares of other and, in this process, has cut the profitability of all.

4. Declining Industry: After the maturity of an industry, it may start showing declining trend in its total market size. This may happen either because of decline of society's needs for the product or availability of substitute product or both. For example, while cloth washing need of the society has remained the same, demand for oil-based laundry soaps has diminished fast because of their replacement by synthetic-based washing system. When a new product emerges as a substitute to an old product, a fresh cycle begins. In a declining industry, competitors do not go for any additional differentiation and competitive advantages as they see no opportunity in these. Many of the prefer either to leave the market or come out with emerging products.

5. Global Industry: A global industry is one in which the strategic position of competitors in major geographic or national markets are fundamentally affected by their overall global positions. A global firm (often called multinational or transnational) operates in more than one country offering similar products and enjoy certain competitive advantages over domestic competitors because of differentiation based on cost, quality, product features, brand image, or other features. With the liberalization of world economy, more and more industries are becoming global.

Industry Structure

Industry structure essentially means the underlying economic and technical forces operating in an industry.

When number of sellers and type of product differentiation are combined together, there are five types of industry structure:

1. Pure monopoly,
2. Pure oligopoly,
3. Pure competition,
4. Differentiated oligopoly, and
5. Monopolistic competition.

Each type of industry provides different types of opportunities and threats and requires different types of strategic approaches. Let us see how these take place.

Pure Monopoly: Pure monopoly is characterized by the situation in which there is only one seller in the market. Therefore, he decides the marketing conditions including its performance. For an organization to continue as a monopoly in the long run, there must be factors which prevent the entry of other organizations in the field. Since there is only one seller, product differentiation is not required. Usually, such organizations exist in public sector engaged in utilities. Indian Railways at the centrally level and State Electricity Boards at state levels are examples of such organizations.

Pure Oligopoly: The term oligopoly comes from the Greek words *oligos* and *polis* and literally means few sellers. There are few sellers in pure oligopoly and there is no product differentiation by these sellers. However, there is no precise limit on the number of sellers that an industry can have to be characterized as pure oligopoly. The key issue is not the number of sellers but the reaction of sellers to one another. Since the product is not differentiated, any price change by one seller affects other sellers because demand is price elastic apart from other determinants of demand. Pure oligopoly exists in some industries, for example, in heavy commercial vehicle industry in India, there are two players—TELCO and Ashok Leyland. Therefore, both these compete on price and location basis.

Pure Competition: Pure competition, also known as perfect competition, is characterized by the existence of large number of sellers offering the same product. Since product differentiation is not possible, product price plays a significant role in the industry. Further, since determination of the product price is not within the control of a single seller, the higher profit emerges due to better operational efficiency rather than strategic focus. Most of the commodity industries like sugar, steel, loose tea, etc. fall in this category.

Differentiated Oligopoly: A differentiated oligopoly exists where number of sellers in the industry is limited but they offer product which can be differentiated from others. Such differentiation can be made on the basis of additional product features, styling, quality, delivery, after-sales service, price, etc., depending on the nature of the industry concerned. Passenger car industry is a kind of oligopoly in which number of competitors is very limiter and each competitor position its cars on some unique selling propositions though most of the cars falling in a price band have same functionality. Similar is the case with many other consumer durables like white goods or mechanized farm equipment. Even some companies operating in undifferentiated oligopoly try to move through product differentiation to a limited extent. For example, TISCO has extended its production process to have more value-added products and it differentiates these based on the value addition.

Monopolistic Competition: Monopolistic competition is characterized by the existence of a large number of sellers in a product group with each seller differentiation its product on some basis from that of others. Monopolistic competition has a combination of both monopoly and pure competition. It has the elements of monopoly because the product is differentiated in such a way that it has very high customer loyalty and the company concerned can operate on the basis of monopoly. It has the elements of pure competition as there are numerous sellers which operate in the same product group. The basis focus for competing in a monopolistic competition industry is to put emphasis on product differentiation which ultimately determines the profit performance of a company. Most of the consumer industries with branded products fall in this category.

Thus, five forces shaping competition are:

1. Threats of entry,
2. Bargaining power of buyers,
3. Bargaining power of suppliers,
4. Substitute products, and
5. Rivalry among competitors.

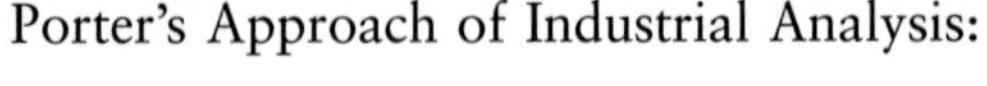
Porter's Approach of Industrial Analysis:

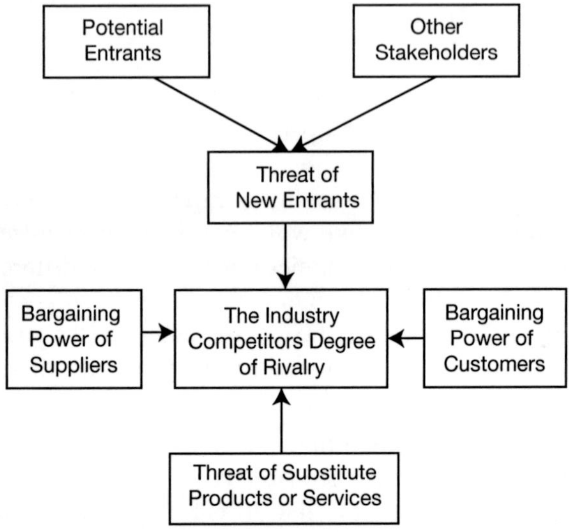

Porter's Approach

Porter contends that an organization is most concerned with the intensity of competition within its industry the degree of this intensity is as shown in the diagram. According to Porter, the collective strength of these forces determines the ultimate profit potential of the industry where profit potential is measured in terms of the long run return on investment of capital. An organization has to assess the importance of each of the following forces for its success:

- Threat of new entrants
- Degree of rivalry among existing firms
- Threat of substitute products or services
- Bargaining power of buyers
- Bargaining power of suppliers
- Relative power of other stakeholders.

The strength of each of these forces determines the ability of the company to raise prices and earn higher profits, for example, in the diagram a strong force can be regarded as a threat since it may reduce profits. A weak force can be viewed as an opportunity as it may allow the company to earn higher profits in the short run, these forces can act as a constraint. However, in the long run, through strategic change, an organization can change the strength of one or more of these forces to its advantage.

Probable impact			
High	medium	low	
High Priority	high priority	medium priority	High
High Priority	medium priority	low priority	Medium
Medium Priority	low priority	low priority	Low
issues priority matrix			

The strategist can rate each competitive force as high, medium or low in strength in relation to a particular industry, for example, if we take the software industry, rivalry can be rated as high. The threat of potential entrants is high, the threat of substitutes is also high. The bargaining power of the supplier is decreasing, i.e. it goes from medium to low. On the contrary, the bargaining power of buyers is increasing from medium to high trends in each of these competitive forces help in assessing the intensity of competition in the industry as a whole.

Porter's model provides a comprehensive framework for industry analysis to develop competitive strategies. The industrial structure is a strong influencer of the rules of the game as well as the potential strategies available to an organization. Competition according to Porter is deep rooted in the underlying economic structure and goes beyond the current competitors behavior. We shall now discuss each of the forces in Porter's model.

Number of Competitors

The degree of rivalry among different firms is a function of the number of competitors, industry growth rate, asset intensity, product differentiation and exit barriers. The number of competitors and industry growth are the most influential of these industries having high fixed costs are likely to face price wars, when the market stagnates or overcapacity becomes a regular phenomenon. Difficulties in exiting from a business also intensifies competition, examples are steel and cement industries.

Threat of Entry

New entrants may increase competition intensity in mature market situations during introduction and growth stages, entry of new firms can help in expanding the market. Mature market situations are characterized by entry barriers, high capital intensity, proprietary technology, etc., for example in the material handling industry, idlers and rollers needed for conveyor belts resulted in the entry of large number of small manufacturers. But this led to price wars. Well established industries in a field due to exit barriers also face profit crunch.

According to Porter intensive rivalry is related to the presence of the following:

- Number of competitors
- Rate of industrial growth
- Product or service change
- Fixed cost
- Capacity
- Exit barriers
- Diversity of rivals

Threat of Substitute Products

A substitute may appear different but may satisfy the same needs as another product; example—Bisleri, Aquafina and Kinley.

According to Porter, "substitutes limit potential returns on the investment by placing a ceiling on the prices, which firms in the industry can profitably charge". As long as switching costs are low substitution can have a strong effect. For example, tea can be considered as a substitute for coffee. Suppose the price of coffee increases, then slowly the coffee drinkers will switch over to tea except, of course, the coffee addicts. We can to a certain extent say that the price of tea puts a price ceiling on the price of coffee, identifying a possible product or service as a substitute is not an easy task, though the product may perform the same function.

Bargaining Power of Buyers

This refers to the ability of the industry's customers to force down prices, bargain for higher quality or more services and play competitors against each other. A buyer or a buyer group is powerful if

- A buyer purchases a large portion of the sellers product or services,
- A buyer can resort to backward integration by producing the product,
- Alternative sources of supply are available,
- Switching costs are low, and
- Purchased product can be easily substituted without affecting the final product, e.g. filament lamp.

Bargaining Power of Suppliers

Bargaining power of suppliers refers to a situation where suppliers can force buyers to pay higher prices and affect their profitability. This would happen when

- Supplier enjoys monopoly.
- Switching costs of buyer are high.
- Substitutes are not readily available, e.g. electricity.
- Suppliers can integrate forward and compete directly with their present customers, e.g. intel can make personal computers.

Relative Power of Other Stakeholders

These groups may be government, local communities, industries, and trade associations, shareholders, special interest groups and creditors not included with suppliers. Importance of these stakeholders varies according to industry. For some industries/projects environmental groups may be important, e.g. power projects.

The collective strength of these six forces determines the attractiveness of the industry, the strongest among these forces becomes the focal point in the formulation of the strategy. For example, TELCO had identified the threats from the suppliers, timely decisions on backward integration helped it to remain competitive.

PORTER'S APPROACH

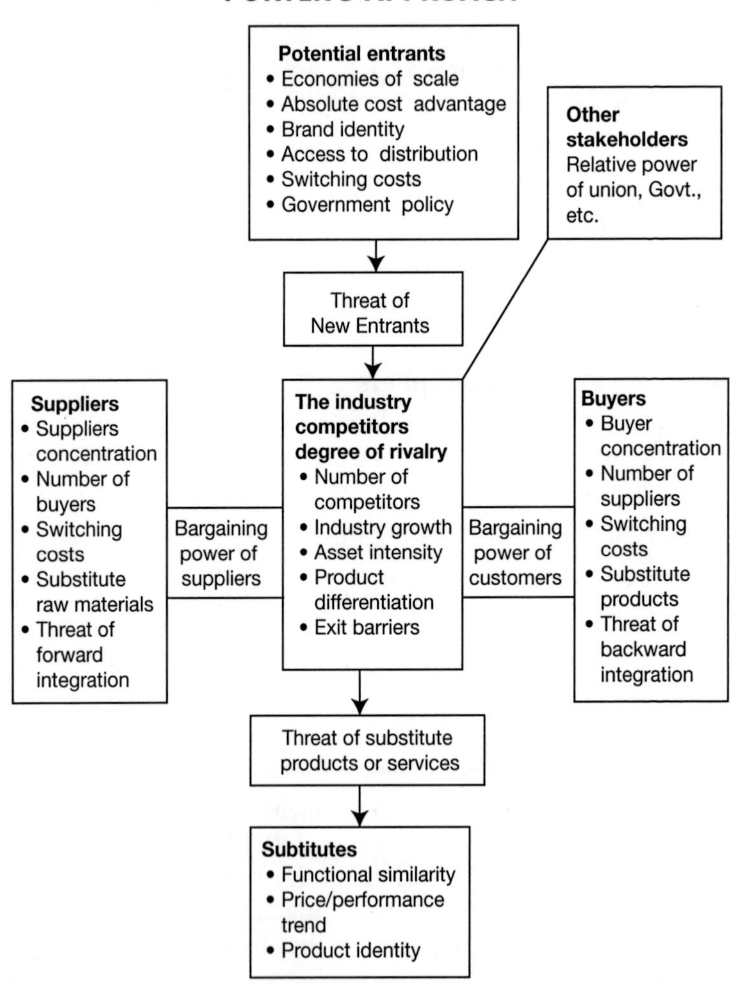

Forces Driving Industry Competition

5.8(e) *COMPETITOR ANALYSIS*

Analysis of forces shaping competition in an industry is basically industry approach of analyzing competition. This must be supplemented by competitor analysis because the outcome of fight for market share is ultimately determined by competitors' behaviour. In an industry, competitors are those companies that satisfy the same customer need, for example, all companies in soft drink industry attempt at satisfying the same customer need though their product positioning may differ. In analyzing competitors, a company faces two types of issue:

1. Identification of competitors, and
2. Competitors' approach.

Identification of Competitors

In an industry, there may be several types of competitors depending on the industry structure. Porter has grouped various competitors into three classes based on three dimensions: strong or weak, close or distant, and good or bad. A strong competitor is one which holds substantial strategic advantages and substantial market share in an industry. A weak competitor is one which does not have any specific strategic advantage and acts as a follower. A close competitor is one which resembles with another company. A distant competitor is one which operates in the same industry group but differentiates its product offerings. A good competitor is one which adheres to industry norms and rules; it is not involved in unreasonable price cutting of similar other tactics to gain market share. A bad competitor is one which tries to buy market share rather than to earn it; it takes large risk by creating overcapacity to upset industry equilibrium. Such a competitor may be called as aggressive one. It is not desirable to name companies in these two categories because of ideological connotation but there are many such companies.

Competitors' Approach

After identifying the companies, their approach in competing in the industry should be analysed. For analyzing competitors' approach, Wall and Shin have identified the various factors on the basis of which a competitor may be analysed. These factors are: pricing, expansion plans, competitive plans, promotional strategy, cost data, sale statistics, research and development, product styling, manufacturing processes, patents and infringements, financing and executive compensation.

5.8(f) *ETOP*

ETOP is the acronym for "Environmental Threat and Opportunity Profile". It is nothing but a summarized picture of the environmental factors and their likely impact on the organization. ETOP is generally prepared in the following manner.

List Environmental Factors

List the different aspects of the relevant environment. For example, economic environment may be divided into rate of economic growth, national income, savings, investment, rate of inflation, capital market reforms, fiscal policy, monarchy policy, etc.

Assess Importance of Environmental Factors

At this stage, the importance of each environmental factors is assessed closely and expressed in qualitative (high, medium or low) or quantitative factors (3, 2, 1). It is worth mentioning here that not all the identified environmental factors will have the same degree of importance.

Assessing the impact: A relevant factor so analysed might have a positive or negative impact as a threat.

Combine to get a bigger picture: In the final stage, the importance of each factor and its impact is compared to produce a compact overall picture.

The preparation of an ETOP helps a firm to identify the segments in a chosen field of activity, presenting excellent growth opportunities. The firm can find out where it stands in the field in comparison to its rivals. Depending on its manufacturing capabilities, technological strength, brand image and distribution network, the firm can think of getting into the 'niche' segment at an appropriate time.

5.8(g) *FORECASTING TECHNIQUES*

Micro environmental and industry scanning and analyses are only marginally useful if all they do is reveal current conditions to be truly useful; such analysis must forecast future trends and changes. Forecasting is a way of estimating the future events that are likely to have a major impact on the enterprise. It is a technique whereby managers try to predict the future characteristics of the organizational environment and hence make decisions today that will help the firm deal with the environment of tomorrow. Although forecasting is an inexact science, four techniques can be particularly helpful: Time Series Analysis, Judgmental Forecasting, Delphi Technique and Multiple Scenarios.

- **Time Series Analysis:** This is an empirical procedure in which certain historical trends (such as population growth, technological innovations, changes in incomes etc.) are used to predict such variable as a firm's sales or market share. Because time series analysis projects historical trends into the future, its validity depends on the similarity between past trends and future conditions (Bright and Schoeman).
- **Judgemental Forecasting:** This is a forecasting technique in which employees, customers, suppliers and/or trade associations serve as a source of qualitative information regarding future trends. For instance, sales representatives many be asked to forecast sales growth in various product categories based on their interaction with customers. Survey instruments may be mailed to customers, suppliers or trade associations to obtain their judgements on specific trends.
- **Delphi Technique:** This is a forecasting procedure in which experts in the appropriate field of study are independently questioned about the probability of some event's occurrence. The responses of the experts are compiled and a summary is sent to each expert. This process is repeated until consensus is arrived at regarding a particular forecasted event.

- **Multiple Scenarios:** Future events can't be predicted easily as our assumptions may go wrong, trends may change, events may take a different route altogether or some unexpected things may change the whole scenario. To overcome these, a manager should formulate several alternative descriptions of future events and trends (called as multiple scenarios).

Other Techniques

Some of the more popular ones in this category include (Bright and Milton) the following:

- **Expert Opinion:** Knowledgeable people are selected and asked to assign importance and probability ratings to various possible future developments. The most refined version, the Delphi method, puts experts through several rounds of event assessment where they keep refining their assumptions and judgements.
- **Dynamic Modeling:** Researchers build sets of equations that attempt to describe the underlying system. The coefficients in the equations are fitted through statistical means. Econometric models of more than three hundred equations, for example, are used to forecast changes in the US economy.
- **Cross-impact Analysis:** Researchers identify a set of key trends (those high in importance and/or probability). The question is then put: "If event A occurs, what will be the impact on all other trends?" The results are then used to build sets of "domino chains," with one event triggering others.
- **Demand/Hazard Forecasting:** Researches identity major events that would greater affect the firm. Each event is rated for its convergence with several major trends taking place in society and for its appeal to each major public group in the society. The higher the event's convergence and appeal, the higher its probability of occurring. The highest-scoring events are then researched further.

After implementing the environmental analysis process, management should continually evaluate and strive to improve it. The process, as pointed out by Certo and Peter, "should be linked to current planning operations, responsive to the information needs of top management, supported by key managers and performed by people who understand the difference between being an analyst and being a strategist".

5.8(h) *SCENARIO BUILDING*

The environments surrounding most firms are varied, complex and challenging. It is not easy to present the collected data in a simple, easy-to-understand format. Scenario building is a useful way of solving this complexity. Scenarios are stories about what the future environment might hold and how a firm might respond to this future. Scenario's help strategies in focusing attention on the emerging picture after thoroughly analyzing the pros and cons of a particularly situation by integrating objective and subjective parts of various factors. Scenario help managers to predict how things will turn out, explain what forces will shape the future and have a feel for the situations that are likely to unfold. Scenarios can be developed thus (Pearce & Robinson).

- Prepare the background by assessing the overall social environment under investigation (such as social legislation).
- Select critical indicators and search for future events that may affect the key trends (e.g., growing distrust of business).
- Analyse reasons for past behavior for each trend (e.g., perceived disregard for air and water quality).
- Forecast each indicator in at least three scenarios, showing the least favourable environment, the likely environment and the most favourable environment.
- Write the scenario from the viewpoint of someone in the future and describe conditions then and how they developed.
- Condense the scenario for each trend to a few paragraphs.

There are several guidelines for developing useful scenarios. (Simpson)

(1) Avoid focusing exclusively on controllable issues. Scenarios generally present alternative views of uncontrollable developments—not simply lay out the plans and outcomes of internally controlled decisions.

(2) Actively seek out contrarian views. Scenario building compels managers to bring in outsiders with fresh perspectives who will invariably raise questions regarding things insiders may take for granted.

(3) Do reality check as scenarios begin to form. Are the scenarios relevant for the line managers who will decide the firm's future success? Scenarios should address worries that keep line managers up at night. If they do not, they remain pious, academic intentions with little tangible rewards.

(4) Don't get bogged down in too many scenarios or too many details. A scenario is not supposed to capture everything and present a complex picture to the management. The purpose of scenarios, it is worth reiterating again, is to describe different worlds, not to detail all the outcomes possible in the same world.

Chapter 6

Strategic Choice

6.1 MEANING

Strategists collect and evaluate information to assess strengths and weaknesses of the internal environment an opportunities and threats of the external environment. Such an assessment presents a list of possible strategic alternatives. From among those alternatives, choices are made. Strategic choice addresses the question "*where shall we go*". It determines the characteristics and form of an organization's strategic direction.

6.2 DEFINITION

According to Glueck and Jauch, strategic choice is "the decision to select among the grand strategies considered the strategy which will best meet the enterprise's objectives". It involves, basically, four steps:

(a) Focusing on a few alternatives,

(b) Determining the selection factors,

(c) Evaluating alternatives and,

(d) Making the strategic choice.

6.3 CRITERIA FOR STRATEGIC CHOICE

6.3(a) *GAP ANALYSIS*

It focuses management's attention on the difference between what was intended and what was achieved. If a firm is not able to achieve its stated objectives through an existing strategy, it must try to bridge the gap through an alternative course of action.

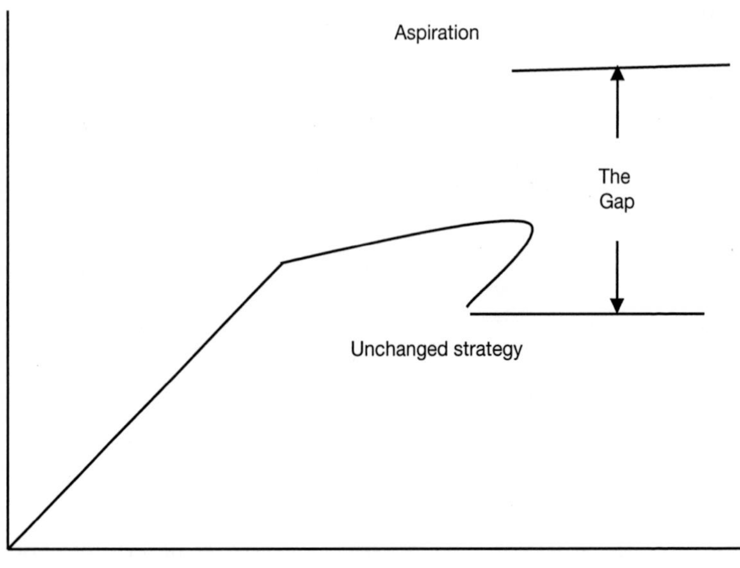

Gap analysis compels managers to measure their performance and to audit their gap closing capabilities (Karni) through soul-searching questions such as: what are the current objectives and what are our future aspirations in terms of profit, growth, market share etc.? Are our results adequate? Are we working hard enough? Are we over reaching? Should our strategy or objectives be changed? As the figure indicates, gap analysis compares achievement with aspiration. In this example, the future sales of the firm, if it pursues its current strategy unchanged, (the bold line), appear likely to fall, although management is keen on very substantial growth (the dotted line). The gap is the difference between target and likely achievement.

If the gap is negative, as in figure, we may wish to consider whether our resources, including our competencies and competitive advantages, are up to the task. A more modest ambition might be more rewarding and less risky, because it is feasible. Alternatively, we might seek projects, programmes, and strategies to close the gap, as Ansoff suggests. If the gap is positive and performance exceeds aspiration, we should consider the merits of revising objectives upwards (expansion strategies). If the gap is negative due to bad performance, certain hard decisions should be taken (retrenchment strategies).

6.3(b) *BUSINESS DEFINITION*

In deciding on what would be a manageable number of alternatives, it is advisable to start with the business definition. Business definition, as discussed earlier, determines the scope of activities that can be undertaken by a firm. It tries to answer three basic questions clearly:

(1) Who is being satisfied?

(2) What is being satisfied?

(3) How the need is being satisfied?

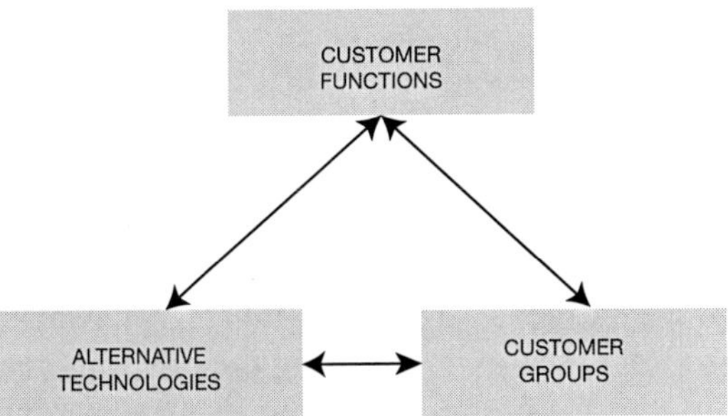

The three dimensions along which a business is defined help a strategist to chalk out alternatives in a systematic manner. Using a business definition, a toilet soap manufacturer may develop strategic alternatives by posing certain questions

- Should the focus be on premium soaps, popular soaps or discount soaps?
- If the focus is on premium soaps, what type of customer functions and service offerings should receive careful attention? (such as flavor, fragrance, fatty acid content, packing, pricing, promotion campaigns, etc.)
- Where should the product be tested initially? (Northern region, Western region, Southern region, etc.)

6.4 SELECTION FACTORS DETERMINING STRATEGIC CHOICE

Following are the various factors available for determining strategic choice:

Objective, analytical tools	Subjective factors
1. BCG Portfolio Matrix	1. Commitment to Past Strategies
2. GE Multifactor Portfolio Matrix	2. Attitudes Toward Risk
3. Product-Market Evolution Matrix	3. Degree of the firm's external dependence
4. Directional Policy Matrix (DPM)	4. Internal Political Considerations
5. Arthur D.Little Portfolio Matrix	5. Time Constraints
6. Strategic position and Action Evaluation	6. Corporate culture
7. Profit impact of market Strategy (PIMS)	

6.4(a) *BCG PORTFOLIO MATRIX*

The BCG Matrix compares various businesses in an organization's portfolio on the basis of relative market share and market growth rate. Relative market share is determined by the ratio of a business's market share (in terms of unit volume) compared to the market share of its largest rival. Market growth rate is the growth in the market during the previous year relative to growth in the economy as a whole. The combination of high and low market share and high and low business growth rate provide four categories for a corporate portfolio (Hedley, Naylor).

Market Growth Rate

	High	Low
High	Stars	Question marks
Low	Cash cows	Dogs

Relative Market Share

Stars

SBU that are stars have a **high share and a high-growth market** and typically require large amounts of cash to support their rapid and significant growth. They have additional growth potential and so profits should be ploughed back into this business for future growth and profits.

For example, software, entertainment, electronics and telecommunication are some of the industries which have a very high growth rate. The appropriate strategy for stars is to maintain the market share through large doses of investment (both internal as well as external).

Cash Cows

SBU's that are 'cash cows' (provide lot of cash for the firm) have a **high market share in a slowly growing market.** As a result, they tend to generate more cash than is necessary to maintain their market position. Cash cows are often former stare and can be valuable in a portfolio because they can be 'milked' to provide cash for other riskier and struggling businesses.

Question Marks (problem child or wild cat)

SBUs that are 'question marks' have a **small share of a high growth market.** The question mark business is risky, since there is already a leader in that business. As such it requires lot of funds to invest in plant, equipment and personnel in order to keep pace with the fast-growing market. The terms question mark is well conceived, because at every stage the organization has to think hard about whether to keep investing funds in the business (to turn it into a star) or to get out.

Dogs

SBUs that are 'dogs' have a relatively **small share of a low-growth market.** They may barely support themselves, or they may even drain cash resources that other SBUs have generated. Usually dogs are harvested, divested or liquidated (if turnaround is not possible).

Four basic strategies can be formulated while building a balanced portfolio:

- Heavily invest in Stars. High market share and high industry growth mean higher probability of future success.

- Maintain cash cows because they provide resources for future growth-investment in wild cats and stars.
- Use selective resource allocation for wildcats to convert them into stars.
- Liquidate or divest dogs that are not worth investing in to improve their position.

Shortcomings of BCG Matrix

The BCG Matrix suffers from a number of shortcomings:

(1) It does not directly address the majority of businesses that have average market shares in markets of average growth (the matrix talks about only two categories, high and low for each dimension).

(2) Generalizations based on the model also may be misleading, since organizations with low market shares may not necessarily be question marks. For example, in India the Ford Ikon, Mitsubishi Lancer managers may raise car production only after careful debate, lest the models lose their exclusive image.

(3) Likewise, businesses with large market shares in slow growth markets may not necessarily be cash cows because they may actually need substantial investments to retain their market position.

(4) The matrix, further, does not offer guidance regarding which question marks to support and which dogs to salvage.

(5) The terminology used is somewhat you are an ugly duckling, much worse to be told explicitly that you are.

(6) The data to position products/SBUs accurately on the matrix are not always available.

(7) Finally, growth and market share are not the only factors which make markets attractive and which give companies strength in markets.

6.4(b) *GE MULTI-FACTOR PORTFOLIO MATRIX*

General Electric Company has developed a 3*3 business portfolio matrix in the 1970s with the help of Mckinsey and Company (also called GE Business Screen or Mckinsey Screen).

In this matrix there are two dimensions:

- Industry attractiveness (similar to BCG's industry growth rate), and
- Relative business strength (similar to BCG's market share).

Industry attractiveness is measured by a number of factors like size of market, market growth rate industry profitability, competitive intensity cyclicality, economies of scale, technological requirements, etc.

Likewise relative business strength is rated considering a number of factors such as market share, profit margins ability to compete on price and quality, knowledge of customer and market competitive strengths and weaknesses, technological capability and caliber of management. These two dimensions make excellent marketing sense for rating a business.

Companies will be successful if they enter attractive markets with required business strengths. If one or the other is missing, the firm may fail to deliver the goods.

Neither a strong company operating in an unattractive market nor a weak company operating in an attractive market will do well.

Both the dimensions (industry attractiveness and relative business strength) are further divided into three zones having nice cells.

The shaded cells at the upper left include the strong SBUs in which the company should invest and grow.

The diagonal cells contain SBUs that are medium in overall attractiveness. The company should maintain its level of investment in these SBUs.

The three shaded cells at the lower right indicate SBUs that are low in overall attractiveness. The company should seriously think of harvesting or divesting those SBUs.

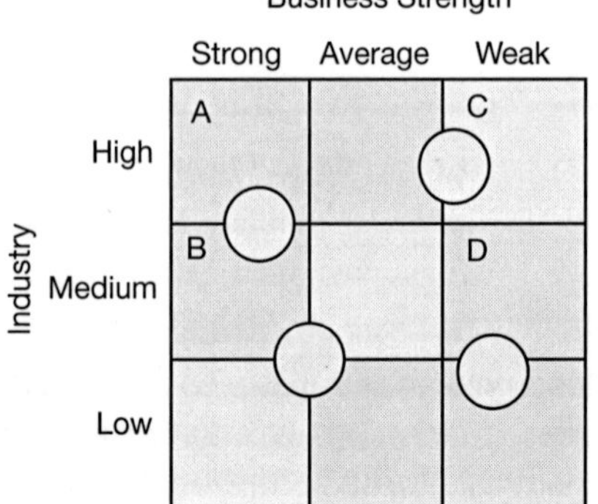

Circle A shows a company SBU with a 75 per cent market share in a good sized, highly attractive industry in which the company has strong business strength.

Circle B represents an SBU that has a 50 per cent market share, but the industry is not very attractive.

Circles C and D indicate two other company SBUs industries where the company has small market shares and not much business strength.

6.4(c) *PRODUCT/MARKET EVOLUTION MATRIX*

A weakness in GE approach has been identified by Hofer and Schendel. They suggest that this approach does not depict the positions of businesses that are about to emerge as winners because the product is entering the take off stage, in order to overcome this problem, they have constructed a fifteen-cell matrix taking competitive position and stages of product/market evolution dimensions. This matrix is presented in figure.

	Competitive Position		
	Strong	Average	Weak
Development		A	
Growth	B		C
Shakeout		D	
Maturity saturation	E		
Decline			F

Various businesses of an organization can be shown on this matrix taking into account their competitive position and stages of product/market evolution and the future of these businesses can be determined. Accordingly, business a would appear to be a developing winner, business B may be classified as a potential winner, business C can be developed into future winner by improving its competitiveness, business D may be labeled as established winner, business E may be cash cow, business F may be called a loser or dog and so on. Thus, the following conclusions can be drawn:

1. Businesses falling in strong competitive position and in development and growth market may be future winner.
2. Businesses falling in average competitive position and in development and growth market may be converted into future winner by increasing their competitive position.
3. Businesses falling in weak competitive position in any market, particularly more son mature and declining market are potential losers. Therefore they can be considered for divestment.
4. Businesses falling in strong competitive position and in mature and shakeout markets may be termed as cash cows because of their ample cash generating capacity.
5. Businesses falling in average competitive position and in saturated and declining markets can also be candidates for future divestment.

6.4(d) *DIRECTIONAL POLICY MATRIX (DPM)*

Directional Policy Matrix (DPM), developed by shell chemicals, UK uses two dimensions—business sector prospects and company's competitive capabilities—to choose strategies. Each dimensions is further divided into 3 degrees—businesses sector prospects into unattractive, average, and attractive and company's competitive capabilities into week, average and strong. The combination of two dimensions with three degrees of each gives nine cells as shown in the diagram.

Business Sector Prospects

Competitive capabilities	Unattractive	Average	Attractive
Weak	Divestment	Phased withdrawal	Double or quit
Average	Phased withdrawal	Custodial	Try harder
Strong	Cash generation	Growth	Market leadership

In this diagram each quadrant shows the type of strategy, the organization may adopt. The keywords used are briefly explained below:

(1) Divestment

A business with weak capability and unattractive business prospect usually incurs losses at the present and the situation is likely to continue in future too. Therefore, such a business should be divested and resources released should be utilized in other businesses.

(2&4) Phased Withdrawal

Such businesses which fall in quadrant 2 with weak capability and average business prospects, or in quadrant 4 with average capability and average business prospects may be divested. In phase as these businesses are not likely to earn enough as compared to other businesses in the portfolio.

(3) Double or Quit

The business which has high business prospects but weak capability may have two alternatives. Either the business is strengthened by allocating additional resources to take the advantages of the alternative business prospects, or if it is not possible to allocate additional resources, it is advisable to divest.

(5) Custodial

The business falling under average capability and average business prospects has two alternatives. Either the organization may bear with the situation and make good the overall position with the help of other businesses, or it may divest thus to concentrate on other businesses.

(6) Try Harder

The business which has average capability but attractive business prospects needs additional resources to strengthen its capability so as to take the advantage of attractive business prospects.

(7) Cash Generation

The business which has strong capability but unattractive business prospects may be used for cash generation and no further investment is required because of unattractive business prospects.

(8) Growth

The business with strong capability and average business prospects requires additional investment in the form of product innovation through R&D and creation of additional production capacity so as to fight in the market to increase the market share.

(9) Market Leadership

The business with strong capability and attractive business prospects may be used to become market leader by allocating additional resources and, once market leadership is established by innovation, to maintain leadership position.

6.4(e) *ARTHUR D. LITTLE PORTFOLIO MATRIX* (ADL)

This life cycle approach postulates that industries classify business units within an organization by industrial maturity and strategic competitive position resulting in the matrix.

The life cycle approach postulates that industries can be grouped into the following stages of maturity.

Embryonic. It is characterized by rapid growth, rapid changes in technology, pursuit of new customers and fragmented and changing shares of market.

Growth. It is characterized by rapid growth, but customers, market share and technology are better known and entry into the industry is more difficult.

Mature. It is characterized by stability in known customers, technology and market shares. The industry can however still be competitive.

Aging. It is characterized by falling demand, declining number of competitors and in many such industries, a narrowing of the product line.

The determination of a business units strategic competitive position calls for a qualitative decisions based on multiple criteria such as

- Breadth of product line,
- Market share,
- Movement in market share, and
- Changes in technology.

The life cycle approach maintains that as these criteria change overtime, a business unit either gains or loses competitive advantage and can be classified as being dominant, strong, favourable, tenable or weak.

Stages of Industry Maturity

Embryonic	Growth	Mature	Aging
Fast grow Start up	Fast grow Attach cost leadership Renew Deland position	Deland position Attain cost leadership Renew Fast grow	Deland position Focus Renew Grow with industry
Start up Differentiate Fast grow	Fast grow Catch up Attain cost leadership	Attain cost leadership Renew Focus Grow with industry	Find niche Hold niche Hang-in Grow with industry Harvest
Start up Differentiate Focus Fast grow	Differentiate Focus Catch up Grow with industry	Harvest Hang-in Find niche Hold niche Renew Turn around Differentiate Focus Grow with industry	Retrench Turn around
Start up Grow with industry Focus	Harvest Hold niche Hang-in Find niche Turn around Focus Grow with industry	Harvest Turn around Find niche Retrench	Divest Retrench
Catch up Grow with industry Find niche	Turn around Retrench	Withdraw Divest	Withdraw

6.4(f) *STRATEGIC POSITION AND ACTION EVALUATION (SPACE)*

Roweetal have developed a model basic on a company's strategic position in comparison to the strategic position of the industry. Called as Strategic Position and Action Evaluation Matrix, the model is based on four important factors;

Internal Strategic Position	External Strategic Position
Financial Strength (FS)	**Environmental Stability (ES)**
Return on investment	Technological changes
Leverage	Rate of inflation
Liquidity	Demand variability
Working capital	Price range of competing products
Cash flow	Barriers to entry into market
Ease of exit from market	Competitive pressure
Risk involved in business	Price elasticity of demand
Competitive Advantage (CA)	**Industry Strength (IS)**
Market share	Growth potential
Product quality	Profit potential
Product life cycle	Financial stability
Customer loyalty	Technological know-how
Competition's capacity utilization	Resource utilization
Technological know-how	Ease of entry into market
Control over suppliers and distributors	Productivity, capacity utilization
A stable environment represents a better strategic position.	Strategic position than an unstable environment.

Strategic position and action evaluation (SPACE) is an extension of two-dimensional portfolio analysis which helps an organization to hammer out an appropriate strategic posture. SPACE involves a consideration of four dimensions.

1. Organizations competitive advantage
2. Organizations financial strength
3. Industry strength
4. Environmental stability.

SPACE FACTORS

Competitive advantage	**Industry strength**
market share	profit potential
product quality	growth potential
product life cycle	financial stability
product replacement cycle	technical know how
customer loyalty	resource utilization
competitions capacity utilization	capital intensity
technical know how	ease of entry into market
vertical integration	productivity, capacity utilization
Financial strength	**Environmental stability**
return on investment	technological changes
leverages	rate of inflation
liquidity	demand variability
capital required and available	price range of competing products
cash flow	competitive pressure
ease of exit from market	price elasticity of demand
risk involved in the business	entry barriers

Various SPACE factors are measured in terms of degrees, often quantified from 0 to 5 with 0 indicating the most unfavourable and 5 indicating the most favourable. Based on these degrees, SPACE diagram is prepared as shown in the diagram.

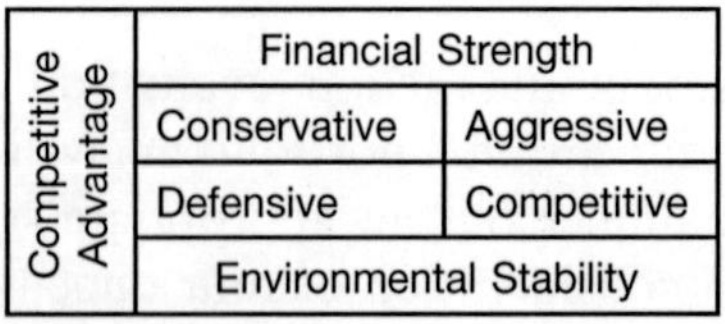

<table>
<tr><td rowspan="4">Competitive Advantage</td><td colspan="2">Financial Strength</td></tr>
<tr><td>Conservative</td><td>Aggressive</td></tr>
<tr><td>Defensive</td><td>Competitive</td></tr>
<tr><td colspan="2">Environmental Stability</td></tr>
</table>

Depending on the nature of four dimensions, organisation's financial strength its competitive advantage, industry strength, and environmental stability, the organization may adopt any of the following strategic postures:

1. Aggressive posture
2. Competitive posture
3. Conservative posture
4. Defensive posture

1. Aggressive Posture

Aggressive posture is adopted when an organization enjoys competitive advantage and has strong financial strength followed by industry attractiveness and stable environment. Such a strategic posture leads to concentric expansion, vertical integration and concentric diversification. For example, Hero Honda has adopted a massive concentric expansion of its motorcycles as all the four dimensions are highly favourable.

2. Competitive Posture

Competitive posture is suitable to an organization which enjoys competitive advantage but has limited financial strength. It operates in attractive industry but has limited financial strength. It operates in attractive industry but environment is relatively unstable. Such a strategic posture leads to concentric merger, conglomerate merger, and turnaround. For example, Bata India operates in such a condition and concentrated more an turnaround and concentric merger to some extent.

3. Conservative Posture

Conservative posture is adopted when an organization has financial strength but has very limited competitive advantage. The industry in which it operates is not attractive though environment is relatively stable. Such a strategic posture leads to stability strategy and conglomerate diversification. For example, TISCO operates in this situation and has concentrated on stability strategy.

4. Defensive Posture

Defensive posture is suitable when an organization has low financial strength and lacks competitive advantage. It operates in an industry which is not attractive and environment is relatively unstable. Such a posture leads to divestment, liquidation, and other forms of retrenchment. For example, most of the jute bag manufacturers operate in such a situation.

Competition Analysis

The ongoing process of liberalization in the country has made it essential for firms to have a very close look at competition. As a strategist, one has to ensure that the organization has competitive advantage in terms of achievement of gials in relation to market share and profitability.

Need to Study Competition

The traditional view of competition focused on the variables of market strategy, such as production quality, keeping delivery schedule, attractive prices and aggressive promotions. The liberalization process has made it essential for firms to go beyond these boundaries. There is a need to understand and answer some of the fundamental questions with regard to "why" and "how". A firm has to consciously answer the following questions:

- What are the drivers of competition in the specific industry?
- What are the anticipated actions of companies in the wake of increased competition?
- In the light of the above, how best can the firm position itself to leverage the competition advantage?

6.4(g) *PROFIT IMPACT OF MARKET STRATEGY (PIMS)*

PIMS was invented by General Electric in the 1960s to examine which strategic factors most influence cash flow and investment needs and success. Its scope was extended by Harvard Business School and subsequently in 1975 the Strategic Planning Institute was set up to develop PIMS for a variety of clients. The Profit Impact of Market Strategy is a computer based model and its data base is information submitted by clients (participating companies) covering the financial and market performance of successful firms and 'real losers' in the market place. The model basically tries to examine the impact of a wide variety of strategic and environmental issues on business performance.

It also offers principles that will help managers to understand how market conditions and specific strategic choices might affect business performance.

Three basic sets of variables have been found to account for 75 to 80 per cent of the variance in profitability and cash flow in the sample of businesses:

(1) the competitive position of the business, as measured by market share and relative product quality;

(2) the production structure, including investment intensity and productivity of operations; and

(3) the relative attractiveness of the served market, comprising the growth rate and customer's characteristics.

Some of the key PIMS findings on the linkage between strategy and performance may be stated thus (Buzzell and Gale).

1. In the long run, the most important factor affecting a business unit's performance is the quality of its goods and services, relative to those of competitors.
2. Market share (relative to the largest competitors) and profitability are strongly linked. There is a linear relationship between market share and profitability. The PIMS study reports that businesses with market shares above 40 per cent earn an average ROI of 30 per cent (this has compelled many firms to increase their market share subsequently). Of course, the study did not say anything about the optimum level of market share—a firm should aim at.
3. High-investment intensity acts as a powerful drag on profitability.
4. While market growth and relative share are linked to cash flows, many other factors also influence performance.
5. Vertical integration (ownership of other firms along a channel of distribution) is a powerful strategy for some kinds of business, but not for all. For small-share

businesses, return on investment is highest when the degree of vertical integration is low. But for businesses with average or above-average share positions, return on investment is highest when vertical integration is either low or high and lowest in the middle.

6. Most strategic factors boosting return on investment also contribute to the long-term market value of a business.

6.4(h) *SUBJECTIVE FACTORS INFLUENCING STRATEGIC CHOICE*

1. Commitment of Past Strategies. Past strategy strongly influences current strategic choice. Current strategies, who have built past strategies through painstaking efforts, do not completely break away from familiar routes. Since they have invested lot of time, resources and energies in developing these strategies, they tend to make a choice that closely parallels or involves incremental alterations to the current strategy.

2. Attitudes toward Risk. Managerial attitudes towards risk are another factor that has a significant bearing on strategic choice. Risk adverse managers prefer to go by past trends and strategies. Where attitudes favour risk, the range of the strategic choice expands. Managers tend to assume aggressive postures and are open to high risk strategies.

3. Degree of Firm's External Dependence. 'If a firm is highly dependent on one or more environmental elements, its strategic alternatives and its ultimate strategic choice must accommodate that dependence'. Firms dependent on large government contracts are more inclined to take decisions in conformity with what the government says ultimately. Multinational companies in India acknowledge that their strategic alternatives are often dictated by national, industrial and economic policies framed by government.

4. Internal Political Considerations. Internal political forces influence strategic choice on many occasions. Dominant coalitions within a company exert lot of pressure when a particular choice affects their functioning in a significant way.

Thus, public sector bank unions have opposed the introduction of computerization process in early 1990s quite vehemently.

5. Time Constraints. The time factor influences the choice of strategies in various ways.

First, the time pressures. When executives do not find time to collect necessary information and consider all possible alternatives, they have to choose a particular course of action based on insufficient data, 'gut' feel, experience, etc.

Second, the time frame of the decision i.e., the short-term and long-term consequences of the decision. If managers are rewarded on the basis of short-term achievements, they tend to discount choices that would enhance shareholder value in the long-term.

Third, the question of time horizon of the decision needs to be looked into. Generally, it is easy to get the support from various quarters where the time horizon is short. The longer a decision can be delayed, the lower the probability that it will ever be accepted.

Finally, the timing of a decision is also important. Prompt decisions enable a firm to encase emerging opportunities quickly. It does not give any room for competitors to give a try and exploit the chances.

When decisions get delayed, the field remains wide open. Threats can come from any corner, substantially diluting the competitive advantage that a firm is able to visualise in a particular area.

6. Competitive Reactions. While weighing strategic choices, top management should also look at how the competitor would react in the immediate future. A massive advertising campaign is likely to alert all competitors in the field and compel them to retaliate with equal force. Posing a threatening challenge to a key competitor would compel the other firm to invade the field with all its forces and mount an aggressive counter strategy.

7. Corporate Culture. Every organization has a culture that puts powerful pressure on the behaviour of managers. The term 'organization culture' here refers to a system of shared meaning (beliefs, feelings, values, etc.) held by members that distinguishes an organization from other organizations. A firm that is used to slow growth and a conservative management style cannot be turned into an aggressive player suddenly. To be more practical, the cultural dimension needs to be taken into account while formulating and implementing the strategy. The strategic choice should be in line with existing managerial philosophy and practices.

Chapter 7

Strategic Formulation

Strategic formulation—input stage, matching stage and decision stage, cultural aspect of strategic choice and functional strategies.

7.1 INTRODUCTION

Formulation of strategy is referred to as strategic planning and is concerned with the development of an organization's mission, objectives, strategies and policies. The starting point is the situation analysis, i.e. SWOT (strengths, weakness, opportunities, threats) analysis. It is also being recently referred to as mapping the business landscape here, we do the SWOT analysis should help in identifying the distinctive competence the organization. This includes the particular capabilities and resources that an organization possesses, the superior way in which they are used and the identification of opportunities that the organization is not able to take advantage of currently due to lack of adequate resources.

7.2 TYPES OF STRATEGY

7.2(a) *INTENDED STRATEGY*

An intended strategy is a planned and deliberate. It is the set of intentional acts that is contemplated and planned to accomplish a good. An intended strategy is also called as deliberate strategy.

It also determines the basic consisting in behaviour and approach of a particular firm towards the economy in general and the market in which it operates in particular.

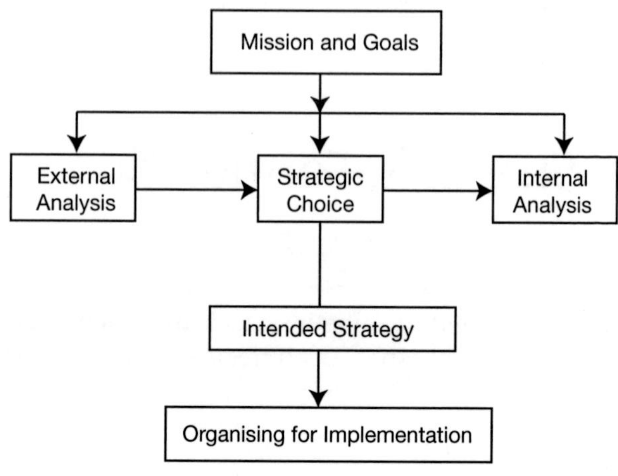

7.2(b) *EMERGENT STRATEGY*

It was the first expert who coined word 'emergent' describing the continuous evolution of corporate strategy of an organization as it not only strived to keep pace with but also attempted to overtake the external environment to reach pre-determined target.

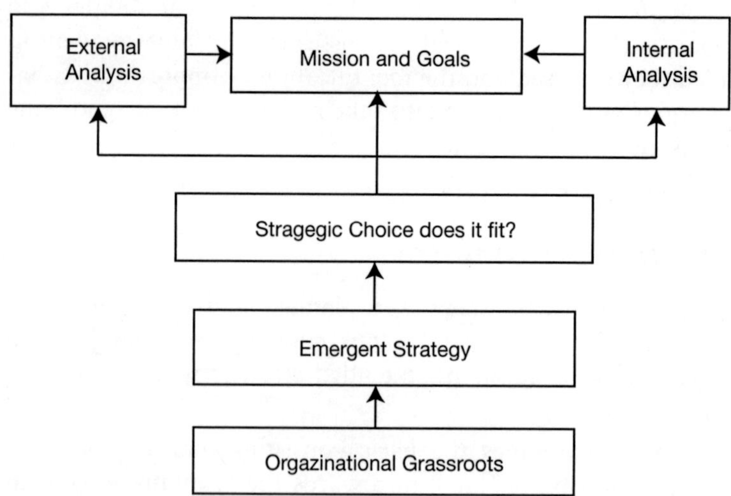

7.2(c) *GENERIC STRATEGY*

Porter's generic strategies describe how a company pursues competitive advantages across its chosen market scope. There are three/four generic strategies either

-Lower cost,

-Differentiation,

-Focus.

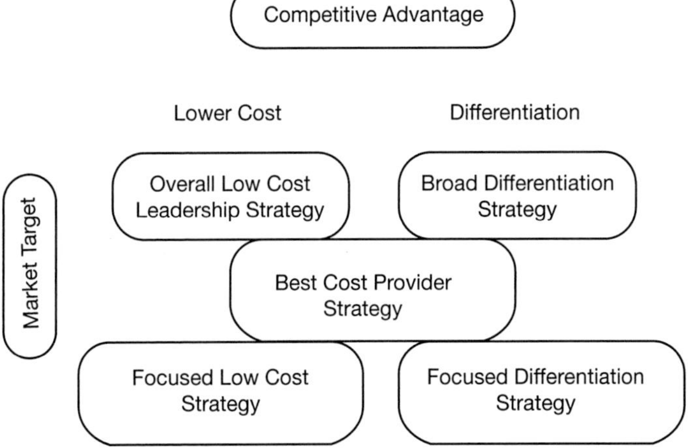

A. Cost Leadership Strategies

Cost leadership is where the organization concentrates on being the low-cost operator in this sector. In order to be able to do this it seeks out all sources of cost advantage. Organization, production, marketing and distribution structures and strategies are all geared up to this key purpose company leadership position by means of the product/market/distinctive competency choices that it makes to gain a low-cost competitive advantage.

B. Differentiation Strategies

Differentiation strategies are those, which seek a uniqueness or identity for their products in ways that are widely valued by buyers other than price advantage. This involves conducting marketing, promotions and public relations activities to give the organization and its offerings a distinctive identity. Firms that can achieve and sustain differentiation are likely to be above average performers in their sectors provided that the price premium more than covers the costs and charges incurred in 'being different'.

C. Focus Strategy

The focus strategy differs from the other two, chiefly because it is directed towards serving the needs of a limited customer group or segment. A focus strategy concentrates on serving a particular market niche, which can be defined geographically, by type of customer, or by segment of the product line. The focus strategy has two variants:

1. Cost focus—where a firm seeks a cost advantage in its target segment.
2. Differentiation focus—where firm seeks differentiation in its target segments.

	Offers products to only one group of customers.	Offers products to many kinds of customers.
Offers low priced products to customers.	Focused cost-leadership strategy.	Cost-leadership strategy.
Offers unique or distinctive products to customers.	Focused differentiation strategy.	Differentiation strategy.

D. Best Cost Provider Strategy

The best cost provider strategy targets the value conscious buyers. It gives customers more value for the money. The product line consists of good-to-excellent attributes, several-to-many upscale features. Marketing emphasis on under-price rival brands with comparable features. The basis of this strategy is unique expertise in managing costs down and product/service caliber up simultaneously.

7.2(d) *GRAND STRATEGY*

Grand strategic alternatives revolve around the question of whether to continue or change the business enterprise is currently in or improve the efficiency and effectiveness with which the firm achieves its corporate objectives in its chosen business sector. Glueck and Jauch identity four grand strategies namely stability, expansion, retrenchment and combination of these three strategies.

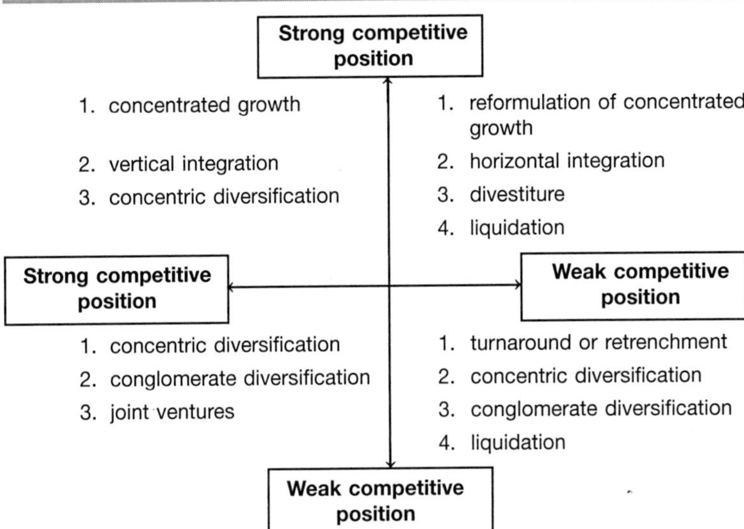

7.2(e) *STABILITY STRATEGY*

Stability strategy means "do the same thing in a better way". It is otherwise known as 'Neutral Strategy'. According to Glueck and Jauch, Stability strategy is a strategy that a firm pursues when there is no scope for significant growth.

7.2(f) *LIQUIDATION STRATEGY*

Liquidation strategy involves closing down a business organization and selling its assets. It is the last alternative strategy as its consequences are severe. The consequences are loss of jobs of all employees, obligations of company towards the stakeholders will be fully or partially unmet and termination of the opportunities of the firm. Liquidation strategy is the most unpleasant and painful, especially for a single business enterprise where it means the organization ceases to exist. For a multi-industry, multi-business firm, to liquidate one of its lines of business is less traumatic.

7.2(g) *COMBINATION STRATEGY*

A company pursues a combination strategy when it adopts more than one grand strategy (i.e., stability, growth and retrenchment) simultaneously or sequentially. During the periods of rapid environmental change, adoption of combination strategy would be necessary. This strategy is common for large scale organizations with multiple units diversified products and national or global markets.

Such firms may liquidate one unit develop another unit and allow the third unit to survive simultaneously to improve the efficiency of the business and maximize the profitability. Once the company's profitability is satisfactory, it may adopt growth strategy. This strategy is also called portfolio restructuring strategy as it is the mix and percentage makeup of different types of businesses in the portfolio.

Company adopts any of the following combinations:

- Stability and growth strategies.
- Stability and retrenchment strategies.
- Growth and retrenchment strategies.
- Growth, retrenchment and stability strategies.

7.3 DIVERSIFICATION

Diversification represents distinctive departures from a firm's existing base of operations, typically the acquisition or internal generation of a separate business with synergistic possibilities counter balancing the two businesses strengths and weaknesses.

The new lines of business may be related to the current business or may be quite unrelated. If the newly added business makes use of the firms existing technology production facilities or distribution channels, it is called as related diversification. Related diversification may take two forms backward integration or forward integration. Some companies expand the business into unrelated industries. This is known as unrelated diversification.

(a) 1950s—General Management skill to manage diversification: There was belief that general management skills provided the justification for diversification. Diversified companies and conglomerates were seen to add value through the skills of their professional top managers, who applied

7.3(a) *CHALLENGES OF DIVERSIFICATION*

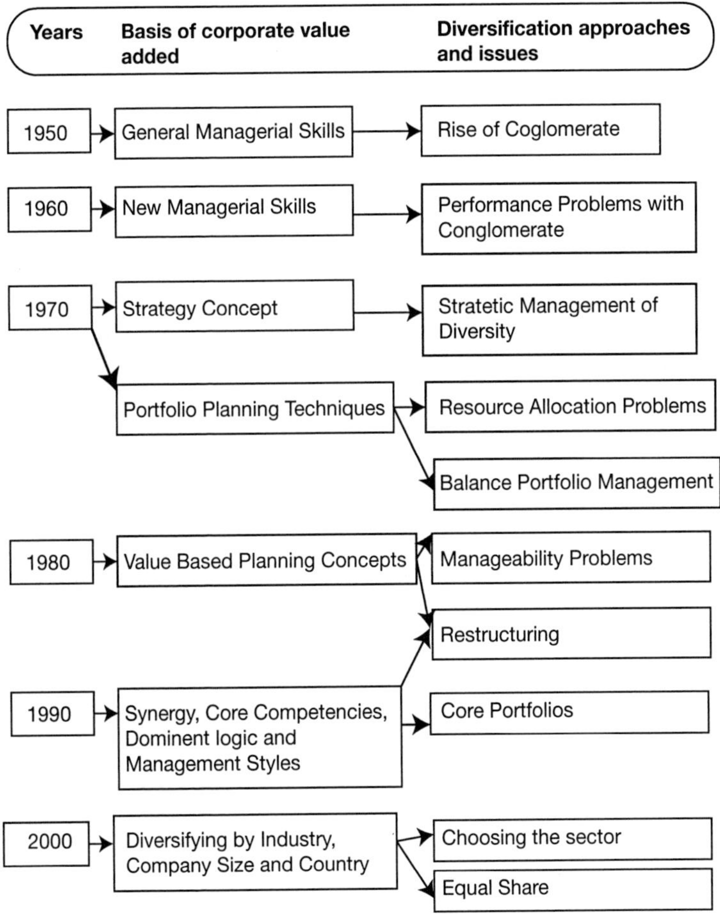

modern management techniques and generalized approaches to a wide variety of businesses across different industries.

(b) 1960s—New Management skill to manage diversification: During the late 1960s, performance of many conglomerates weakened, and a new approach to corporate management of diversity was sought.

(c) 1970s—Portfolio planning techniques to manage diversification: the concepts of strategy and strategic management provided a new focus for senior management's attention during the 1970s. But it did not resolve resource allocation problems as a result portfolio planning techniques were developed. These techniques improved capital allocation across businesses with different strategic positions, and led to balanced portfolio management.

(d) 1980s—Restructuring back to core Business: The above approach overlooked the problem of manageability and so during 1980s poor corporate performance again became a critical issue. The main themes of corporate strategy during the 1980s became restructuring back to core businesses and a resolve to stick to the knitting.

(e) 1990s—Search for synergy and building of core competencies: During 1990s, there is no consensus on what sticking to the knitting in practice implies. Popular themes during this period are search for synergy and building of core competencies. The concept of understanding the dominant strategic logic of a portfolio, and its compatibility with the approaches of top management, seems promising.

(f) Buying stock in many different companies provides a basic level of diversification, but the share number of investments that have is not enough to ensure a high level of diversification. Spreading out investments across large, small and medium-sized companies in different sectors of the economy is key to gain true diversification. Investing in both domestic and foreign assets can avoid betting all of your money on a single country's economy.

7.3(b) *REASONS FOR DIVERSIFICATION*

The following are the reasons for diversification:

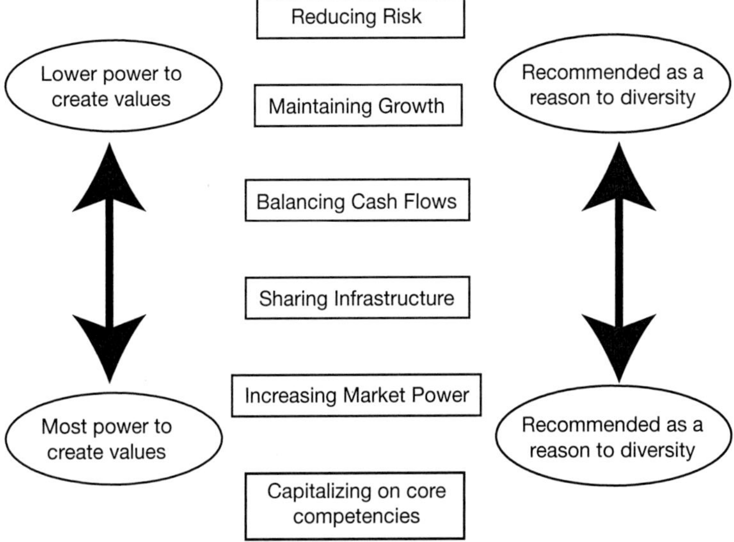

(a) *Risk Minimization*: Some company diversify their business to eliminate or reduce the risks associated with confining the business to one or very few products.

(b) *Growth Maintenance*: Diversification enables companies to better utilize its resources and strengths like technological capabilities, production facilities, managerial expertise, etc. This in turn helps the company to maintain the growth level.

(c) *Balancing Cash Flows*: Diversification encourages the company to share financial resources among the diversified companies helps in achieving effective deployment of funds.

(d) *Increasing Market Power*: Company diversify to by entering the market before the competitors. This strategy increases the power of the company in the market place.

(e) *Capitalizing on Core Competence*: Diversification aims at consolidating the companies market position, image, etc., by capitalizing on core competence.

7.3(c) *TYPES OF DIVERSIFICATION STRATEGIES*

There are six types of diversification strategies, they are:

- Strategies for entering new industries.
- Related diversification strategies.
- Unrelated diversification strategies.
- Corporate turnaround strategies.
- Retrenchment and restructuring strategies.
- Multinational diversification strategies.

The first three diversification strategies mentioned above are ways to diversity; the last three are strategies to strengthen the positions and performance of companies that have already diversified.

Strategies for Entering New Businesses

Entry into new businesses can take any of form.

(a) *Acquisition*

It is the most popular and quicker way to diversify into another industry. Acquiring an already established concern allows the entrant to move directly to the task of building a strong market position in the target industry. One of the big stumbling blocks to entering attractive industries by acquisition is the difficulty of finding a suitable company at a price that satisfies the cost of entry test.

(b) *Internal start-up*

Achieving diversification through internal start-up involves creating a new company under the corporate umbrella to compete in desired industry. The biggest drawbacks to entering an industry by forming a start-up company internally are the costs of overcoming entry barriers and the extra time it takes to build a strong and profitable competitive position.

(c) *Joint venture*

Joint ventures are a useful way to gain access to new business because of the following reasons:

Potential Areas of Co-operation (Win-Win)

Joint venture among the companies with their full satisfaction and co-operation are as under:

- Expanding market access
- Enhanced profitability
- Building competitive advantage
- Access to new technologies
- Increased brand power
- Overall operational synergy
- Greater co-operation through increased awareness of each other.

Potential Areas of Conflict (Win-Lose)

Joint venture is carried on due to the mis understanding and conflict among the companies:

- Management style conflict
- Personality clashes at policy levels
- Varying management control systems
- Culture and value systems
- Conflicting environmental perspectives
- Overlapping brands
- Technology mismatch
- Greater conflict through increased awareness of each other.

Chapter 8

Corporate Level Strategies

8.1 STRATEGIC PLANNING DEFINITION

Strategic planning can be defined as "the continuous process of making present entrepreneurial decisions systematically and with the greatest knowledge of their futurity; organizing systematically the efforts needed to carry out these decisions; and measuring the result of these decisions the expectations through organized systematic feedback".

Strategic planning can be summarized as follows:

- Systematic and purposeful work on attaining objectives to be performed.
- Looking out for a new and different ways of attaining objective rather than continuing the same old method of doing things.
- Deciding time for implementing strategy.

Strategy Plan

Strategic planning is a systematic and disciplined exercise to formulate strategy. It is more comprehensive as it concentrates on the whole organization. Strategic planning is forward looking exercise which determines the future posture of the enterprise. Strategic plans helps in enhancing and sustaining the organizational competitive advantage based on external and internal variables. It is through the plan and organization can accomplish its stated goals using available resources.

8.2 CORPORATE STRATEGIC PLANNING

According to George Steiner, "corporate Strategic planning refers to the formulation of basic organizational mission's purposes and objectives; policies and programs to achieve them; and the methods needed to achieve organizational ends; one framework for formulating and implementing strategies is the formal corporate strategic planning process".

8.3 PURPOSE OF STRATEGIC PLANNING

Corporate strategic planning is concerned with

1. Emphasis is on the future course of action and not day-to-day operations.
2. Business growth characteristics like volume, speed, direction and timing of growth.
3. Environment in which the business operates, and also the interdependencies of both the company and the environment factors.
4. Portfolio of businesses, which include product-market scope and postures.
5. Development of an effective strategy to achieve corporate objectives.
6. Integration of various business functions.
7. Creating core competencies competitive advantages for long-term survival, etc.

8.4 STRATEGIC PLANNING PROCESS

The strategic plan is specific but not detailed, because although specific goals may be established for the distant future, detailed methods for achieving these goals must be related current environment. The strategic plan provides the constraints for selling intermediate and short-term goals. The strategic plan ties together with the development plan (short-range plan). The development plan focuses on the growth of the company through internal or external expansion.

Steps in Strategic Planning Process

The strategic planning process consists of the following steps:

1. Analyze the Environment. It involves identifying those existing and future environmental conditions that have an influence on the company. Environmental scanning is done to identify new opportunities risk to market position and profit margins. Environmental factors include political, economic, social, and technological and market forces.

It is always easier to talk about change than to make it.

—Alvin Toffler

2. Identify Company Strengths and Weaknesses. As a result of environmental analysis along with an orderly review of products, market, processes, personnel and facilities, certain strengths and weaknesses will emerge. Such resource analysis will not serve to highlight possible competitive advantages available to the company to the company but will also tend on opportunities and risks.

3. Personal Values of Top Management. Personal values represent both guides and constraints upon the direction of the business. The aesthetic, religious and personal values of top management and influential stockholders exert significant influences on strategy. The emerging constraints of social responsibility and consumerism are factors that must be considered in strategic planning process.

4. Identify Opportunities and Risks. After considering the above steps, the company should be able to identify the opportunities in the environment to fill a unique niche. These opportunities occur when there are specific needs for products or services that the firm is uniquely able to supply because of its resources.

5. Define Product/Market Scope. This involves the explicit definition of the future scope of the company's activities. The main idea is to concentrate on a very limited number of carefully defined product/market segments. This is advantageous because it

(a) Reduces time and complexity of decisions regarding acquisitions, new investments and other elements of the development plan.

(b) Promotes integration of division and other organizational entities by providing a basis for their plans.

(c) Allows the company to focus on decisions and actions that takes advantages of their competitive edge.

6. Define the Competitive Edge. This requires a careful evaluation of unique company skills, position, market, advantages and other competitive factors.

7. Establish Objectives and Measures of Performance. Quantitative specifications are required to describe many characteristics of the firm and to provide a clear definition of strategy. Quantitative goals may be established for such parameters as annual rate of growth of sales, profits, return on investment, market share, number of employees, standing in the industry and so on.

8. Determine Deployment of Resources. The company should determine the areas, where its resources should be deployed. Conversion from one type of resources to another as changing from labour-intensive to capital-intensive manufacturing is also a part of such deployment.

8.5 MERITS OF CORPORATE STRATEGIC PLANNING

1. Strategic planning helps to envision an organization's future, formulate vision and makes objectives clear.
2. Serves as a framework for systematic handling of corporate decisions.
3. Establishes the objectives of the firm and develops strategies for achieving them.
4. Helps in the choice of firm's businesses, products and markets.
5. Enables each SBU, division, functional department and individuals to understand what is expected out of them.
6. Facilities better delegation, coordination, monitoring, performance evaluation and control.
7. Ensures best utilization of the resources.
8. Helps to overcome the uncertainty resulting from environment disturbances.
9. Build competitive advantages and core competencies.

10. Enable a company to meet competition more effectively.
11. Draw from both "intuition" and "logic".
12. Enhance the problem prevention capabilities of the firm.

8.6 LIMITATIONS OF CORPORATE STRATEGIC PLANNING

1. Strategic planning process is costly and time consuming.
2. It is based on certain premises. If the premises do not hold valid, plans based on them would not be realistic.
3. Complex and dynamic environment makes it difficult to predict the future outcome.
4. Non-adherences to plans results in failure to reach the goals, which causes frustration.
5. Resistance to change affects the implementation of new plans.
6. Lack of commitment at all levels of management results in failure of strategies.

8.7 CORPORATE LEVEL STRATEGY

Meaning

Corporate strategy deals with three key issues facing the corporation as a whole

1. The firm's overall orientation towards growth, stability, or retrenchment (directional strategy)
2. The industries or markets in which markets in which the firm competes through its products and business units (portfolio strategy)
3. The manner in which management coordinates activities, transfers resources, and cultivates capabilities among product lines and business units (parenting strategy)

Corporate strategy is primarily about the choice of direction for the firm as a whole. This is true whether the firm is a small, one-product company or a large multinational corporation. In a large multi-business company, however, corporate strategy is also about managing various product line sand business units for maximum value.

Corporate strategy, therefore, includes decisions regarding the flow of financial and other resources to and from a company's product line and business unit. Through a series of coordinating devices, a company transfers skills and capabilities developed in one unit to other units that need such resources. In this way, it attempts to obtain synergies among numerous product lines and business units so that the corporate whole is greater than the sum of its individual business unit parts. All corporation, from the smallest company offering one product in only one industry to the largest conglomerate operating in many industries with may products must, at one industry to the largest conglomerate operating in many industries with many products must, at one time or another, consider one or more of these issues.

8.8 TYPES OF CORPORATE LEVEL STRATEGY

8.8(a) *MODERNIZATION STRATEGY*

In developing countries like India, technology is often employed as strategic and competitive tool. Modernisation, which basically involves technological upgradation, is used to achieve organizational objectives such as increased production, lower costs, efficiency, productivity, etc. Here, modernisation is dealt with, not in an operational manner indicating technological upgradation, but in a strategic sense. With the respect to the classification of strategic alternatives, modernisation could be considered as:

- Internal stability strategy if the place of modernisation is low to moderate;
- Internal expansion strategy if the place of modernisation is high;
- External expansion strategy if the organization merges with or acquires another company for the purpose of modernisation;
- Internal retrenchment strategy if the resources or redirected from one area to another with aim of modernisation; and

- External retrenchment if the part of the organization is divested or liquidated with aim of the modernisation.

Reasons for Adopting Modernisation Strategy

Modernisation strategies are used for different reasons. As we pointed out earlier, some of these are: increasing production, lowering costs, improving efficiency and productivity, etc. Most of these objectives apparently seem to be aimed at improving the overall performance but they may also be aimed at increasing the competitive ability.

8.8(b) *INTEGRATION GROWTH STRATEGY*

Organization can achieve growth by external integration also. Integration involves joining of two or more organizations together for a common purpose. Integration can be broadly divided into two categories, viz:

(a) *Horizontal Integration*: This involves integration of two or more firms, in the same industry, carrying on the same type of business. This type of integration is carried out to eliminate competition and to gain advantages of economies of large-scale production. Under this arrangement, integrated units are bought under one management. This helps integrated organization to exercise control over the supply of raw materials. They can fix uniform prices.

(b) *Vertical Integration*: This integration results two or more firms, form the same industry, performing different processes of a product join together for a common purpose. In the process of manufacturing a product, there are several processes involved. The processes include acquiring raw material, fabrication of raw material into finished goods and marketing of products. Each of these functions may can be carried out by different firms. Vertical integration helps integrating all these firms together and gain full control from the stage of raw material supply to marketing and distribution of finished goods.

(c) ***Backward Integration***: Backward integration arises when the organization undertakes the preceding stage of the current business. For example, an organization engaged in manufacturing or finished product may start manufacturing raw material needed for the finished product. Another example is that a marketing company, which I currently engaged in the marketing of finished product, may begin to manufacture these products.

(d) ***Forward Integration***: Forward integration arises when the organization undertakes the succeeding stages of the current business. For example, an organization currently engaged in manufacturing, but does not do any marketing, may undertake to market these products. Another example is that a manufacturer of raw material may begin to manufacture finished product using the raw material manufactured by them.

8.8(c) *DIVERSIFICATION GROWTH STRATEGY*

Adding new lines of business to the existing one is called diversification. Under diversification an organization switches over to new products and markets rather than continuing with the existing business alone.

Diversification needs new products, processes, technology, markets and services. Under diversification different products are manufactured and new markets are exploited. The new lines of business intended to be added mayor many not be related to the current business.

Diversification strategy is adopted when the organization finds no more charm or growth in existing business.

(a) Concentric Diversification

The organization may adopt either concentric diversification (related) or conglomerate diversification (unrelated). Concentric diversification results when the organization decides to carry on some other business related to the company's existing line of business.

(b) Related Diversification

Related diversification helps the company to leverage the existing assets, capabilities and strengths to add more value to the business. If a steel manufacturing company enters into iron ore mining, the company is said to have concentric diversification. Using this strategy, organization can leverage its brand name and create stronger capabilities.

(c) Conglomerate Diversification

Conglomerate diversification results when the organization decides to carry on some other business not related to the existing line of business. Conglomerate diversification is adopted when the organization feels that the current industry is unattractive. Spreading business risk across multiple business, optimum use of financial resources, exploiting management capabilities are the distinctive advantages of conglomerate strategies.

8.8(d) *TURN-AROUND STRATEGY*

Turn-around strategy refers to the strategy formulated to turn a sick company into a healthier one. This strategy reverse the declining trends of performance indicators like declining sales, declining market share, decreasing profits, over-manning, high employees turnover, low morale, uncompetitive products, etc.

Before turn-around strategy is introduced the organization must carefully analyze the product, market, production, process, competition, internal management, etc. These factors may include lack of coordination, lack of planning, resistance of CEO towards new ideas and so on. Following the actions suggested for turn-around:

- Change in the top management.
- Quick cost reduction.
- Better internal control.
- Building credibility.
- Neutralizing external pressures.
- Identification of activities giving quick results.
- Liquidation of assets which are not in use to generate cash.
- Developing an appropriate market strategy.
- Financial restructuring.
- Modification of product mix.
- Retrenching excess employees.

- Increasing sales by aggressive marketing and intensive advertising.
- Stopping the manufacturing of marginal products.
- Restricting pricing system.

8.8(e) *DIVESTMENT STRATEGY*

Divestment Strategy involves the sale of those units or part of business that no longer, contribute for the development of the organization. Following are the reasons for divestment:

- Negative cash flow generated by a particular unit causing bad financial implication on the overall activities of the organization.
- If an acquired business is proved to be a big mismatch.
- If technological upgradation is not affordable or possible.
- If the organization finds some other business more profitable than the exciting one.
- If organization feels that it has overgrown and become unmanageable.
- If company feels that there is severe competition to the unit and which cannot be fought back.

8.8(f) *LIQUIDATION STRATEGY*

Liquidation is the act of closing down the activities of a business unit by selling its assets. Management decides to liquidate the business when the organization is making heavy loss in the past many years and if the business unit is not closed now, company may lose its invested capital.

When a company decides to go for liquidation, it should proceed with the sale of assets and settlement of its liabilities.

8.8(g) *MERGER STRATEGY*

A merger occurs when two or more organization join together to avoid competition, to gain advantages of economies of large-scale operations, and to capitalize resources and capabilities of the joining organization. Mergers can take four different forms, viz:

- Horizontal Mergers
- Vertical Mergers
- Concentric Mergers
- Conglomerate Mergers

(a) *Horizontal Mergers*

Horizontal merger is a case where two or more business units carrying on the same business join together for various reasons mentioned earlier. One company manufacturing sugar combines with another sugar manufacturing company is an example for horizontal merger.

(b) *Vertical Mergers (sequence integration)*

According to Prof. Haney, vertical merger "unites organizations which are on different planes and which represents successive stages or trades within an industry. The organizations combined are not competing side by side but stand end to end; one receiving the products of the other as its own material".

From the definition it is clear that vertical merger is the union of the successive stages or processes of manufacture of finished article-beginning from the raw materials; passing through processing to the finished goods and distribution.

For example, in case of sugar industry, the sugarcane cultivation farm may merger with the sugarcane crushing plant, the sugarcane crushing plant with the sugarcane manufacturing plant and the latter may merge with the factory engaged in the manufacture of confectionery, jams, etc.

(c) *Concentric Mergers*

Concentric merger take place when two or more organization related to each other, in terms of customer functions, the alternative technology, combined together.

For example, if a footwear manufacturing company combines with socks making company or with leather goods company making purses, bags, etc.

(d) *Conglomerate Mergers*

Conglomerate merger is the case where a firm in one industry combines with another firm in another unrelated industry. In other words, conglomerate merger arises when two different business are combined together.

For example, footwear company combining with the pharmaceutical company.

Advantages of Mergers

Following are the various advantages of mergers:

1. It helps in elimination or reduction of competition.
2. It helps in gaining advantages of economies of large-scale operations.
3. It helps in the growth of the amalgamating firm.
4. It increases financial strength of the amalgamated firm.
5. It helps in diversification of business (especially in the conglomerate merger).
6. It avoids gestation period of establishing new business. This provides immediate access to the market.
7. Sometimes cost of acquisition may work out to be economical than establishing a new business unit.
8. It helps in achieving synergy. One unit may be strong in financial resources and the other has profitable investment opportunities. Similarly, one unit may have strong brand name but lacks marketing organization. Thus, mergers help in achieving synergy between complimentary activities.
9. It helps in gaining tax benefits. For example, if a company amalgamates with a sick company, set off and carry forward of accumulated depreciation and losses is possible. This reduces income tax burden of the amalgamating company.
10. It helps in procuring resources needed quickly.

Disadvantages of Mergers

Following are the disadvantages of mergers:

1. Merger may result into the acquisition of old plant, outdated technology, etc., from the other company. It may later cause serious problems to the amalgamated company.
2. It must be remembered here that when a business unit is taken over, its problems are also taken over.
3. Sometimes mergers may lead to financial and other problems.
4. If the amalgamating company does not have adequate knowledge about the amalgamated company, management may become a difficult issue.
5. If there is no proper synergy between the companies combined together, merger may turn out to be a failure.

8.8(h) *TAKE-OVER*

- A take-over bid is an offer to purchase enough share of a company to overtake the current majority share holders.
- Assumption of control of another firm through purchase of 51% (or) more of its voting shares or stock.
- In take-over strategy, one company takes over the control of another company. It can be done through the mutual agreement between acquiring and acquired company or against the wishes of the company, known as hostile take-over.

Chapter 9

Strategic Implementation

9.1 INTRODUCTION

Strategy implementation refers to the sum total of the activities and choices required for execution of a strategic plan. It can be referred to as a process by which strategies and policies are put into action by programmes, budgets and procedures. Implementation is a key component of strategic management, strategy formulation and implementation can be considered as two sides of the same coin it is therefore imperative to have a good strategy and a proper implementation the implementation process has to answer the following questions:

- Who will carry out the strategic plan?
- What should be done to align the company's operations in the new direction?
- When and how should everyone concerned respond?

9.2 DEFINITION

According to Steiner, Miner and Gray, "Implementation of strategies is concerned with the design and management of systems to achieve the best integration of people, structures processes and resources in reaching organizational purposes".

9.3 WHO IMPLEMENTS STRATEGY?

The people who implements the strategy are a diverse set, different from those who formulate it. In many large-scale organizations, a large number of people are involved in strategy formulation. The heads of functional areas and their subordinates have to work together for implementation of plans. These plans are spread across departments and units. It becomes imperative on the part of every operational manager down to the employee to get involved in some way in the implementation of the corporate, business and functional strategy.

9.4 ISSUES IN STRATEGY IMPLEMENTATION

The scope of managerial activities associated with strategy implementation is virtually co-existensive with the entire management process. This is obvious because the entire management process is geared up according to the needs of strategy. From analytical point of view, we may classify the various functions relevant for strategy implementation into the following categories:

1. Institutionalization of a strategy through its communication and acceptance, formulation of derivative plans and programmes, translating allocation, activating strategy.
2. Following various procedures to put the strategy in action, i.e., procedural implementation.
3. Design of organization structure and development of organizational system, i.e., structural implementation.
4. Developing plans and policies for different functions, i.e., functional implementation.
5. Developing leadership styles, building organizational climate and infusing values ethical and social consideration, i.e., behavioural implementation.

9.5 ORGANIZATIONAL DESIGN

Efficient performance of activities requires proper organization design/structure. Proper distribution and integration of work is the basic objective of organizational design. The system should provide for proper flow of communication in the organization. Well established authority, responsibility and accountability system must exist in the organization. Organization structure aims at achieve stated objectives effectively with the help of various resources available in the organization. These resources must be properly intertwined to achieve organization success. Organizational design undergo changes based on the internal and external factors. Many Organizations have adopted flat structure in place of tall or vertical structure. Span of control is also expanded. Therefore, organization should respond to the changing environment and adopt a suitable design which would best fit into the organizational strategy. While designing a structure, following steps are to be followed:

Identify various activities that needs to be performed to accomplish the stated objective.

1. Group those activities requiring common skill set.
2. Select an appropriate structure to incorporate different groups of activities.
3. Using these groups, formulate different departments and assign activities and responsibilities.
4. Interrelate various departments for proper co-ordination and communication.

9.6 ORGANIZATIONAL CHANGE

Organization does not exist in vacuum. It is surrounded by ever changing external environment. Changes in the external environment will have a greater impact on the organizational activities. Changing environment may either create an opportunity or pose new threats. Organization must change its structure to use these opportunities and combat threats.

Environment changes may call for structural modification or behavioural modification or both. Structural changes call for use of new technology new methods, new machines, new work system and so on. This necessitates the changes in the earlier system of work. This may lead to new responsibility, new may of work and so on.

Always people resist to changes. They find it difficult to adjust to the changed working environment. This call for behavioural modification of the people working in the organization. If the modified/new strategies or not willfully accepted by the people, strategy may not yield better results. Therefore, it is necessary for the organization to mould the behaviour so that they can take up strategy changes in a positive manner.

9.7 ORGANIZATIONAL SYSTEM

Organization can be viewed as a system of authority and responsibility. Once the authority is delegated and responsibility is fixed, managers must be in opposition to whether the responsibilities are successfully discharged or not. Therefore, there is the necessity for the establishment of various systems for the success of a strategy. The following systems are found necessary for this purpose:

1. Information system
2. Appraisal system
3. Motivation system
4. Control system
5. Planning system
6. Development system

1. Information System: Information is considered as on one of the crucial organization resources. Information is power. Organization must establish on efficiency information system for the supply of necessary information. Organizations use computer based information system (CBIS) for the supply of information. System should supply timely information. Information must be adequate, reliable and relevant, information collected should be properly stored, arranged retrieved and reported to the management for timely action. Information helps in evaluating the performance of different people in the organization. Necessary actions can be initiated to correct the deviations. It will also reveal exceptional performances.

Information system collects information from external environment also. External information is useful for strategic planning. External information reveals market movement, technological changes, nature of competition, etc. These information reveal available opportunities and possible threats in the external environment. Based on these information, organization can formulate strategies and internal strengths to combat threats and capitalize opportunities.

2. Appraisal System: People working in the organization expect praise and raise. They expect appreciation for their excellent work and also the expect increase in their position and remuneration. Therefore, there must be appraisal system established in the organization. Appraisal system must specify what to appraise and when to appraise. The appraisal system must clearly specify the procedure and the prerequisite for an appraisal. Appropriate tools must be adopted for appraisal purpose.

3. Motivation System: Motivation is a process by which behaviour of an individual is aligned with the desired level of organization behaviour. If the desired motivation does not exist in the organization, managers find it difficult to get things done from the people. Organization must provide a system of motivation to influence people to contribute their maximum efforts to the organizational development. Different motivational techniques are available. They may include increase in salary, bonus, profit-sharing, promotion, etc.

4. Control System: Control is established to be the most important management function. Control helps in knowing whether the strategy implementation is in right direction or not. It identifies deviations, if any, and takes correction action before things go out of control. The control system has the following aspects:

(a) Established standards

(b) Measure performance

(c) Compare the actual performance with the standards

(d) Take corrective action.

5. Planning System: Strategic success largely depends on how the plans are formulated to execute these strategies. Planning system should provide scope for participate of people responsibility for implementing these strategies. They must be actively involved at the time of planning stage itself. Participation enhances the probability of success of strategy. Organization must decide whether to have centralized planning system or decentralized planning system. Therefore, planning system must be trailed to suit the desired situation.

6. Development System: Development is defined as the "the process if gradual, systematic improvement of knowledge, skill, performance and attitude of individuals who perform management responsibilities". As stated earlier, the organization has perpetual existence. Continuous changes will keep happening both in the internal and external environment. Managers must be made ready to face these situations. For this, they must be trained to handle various situations. Therefore, organization must formulate strategies for the development of the executives and managers to perform consistently.

9.8 CORPORATE CULTURE

Organization culture can be expected as the complex pattern of beliefs, expectations, ideas, values, attitude and behaviours displayed by the employees of an organization.

The organization culture is determined on the basis of the following:

1. **Individual Initiative.** The culture is largely based on the degree of responsibility, freedom and independence that individuals of the organization have.

2. **Clarity of Objective.** Are the people working in the organization clear about the objectives stated by the organization? If the objective is not clear, positive behaviour cannot be created.

3. **Risk Taking Ability.** Are the people encouraged to take risk? Or are they aggressive and innovative?

4. **Coordination.** Are the people working with close harmony?

5. **Management Support.** Is communication clear? Do the people get sufficient assistance and support from the managers?

6. **Reward System.** Is the reward system based in real performance? Is there any partiality, favoritism? Is the system in place practiced in a justified manner?

7. **Identify.** Do the people identify themselves with the organization or with their work group? It means how attached they are to the organization.

8. **Control.** What is the prevailing control system in the organization? Is close supervision used to control the people?

9. Communication System. Does communication follow formal channel of communication? Is there any scope for two way communication?

Corporate culture has profound influence on the organization success. A strong culture is strength to the organization and a week culture is a hindrance to the organization growth. People working in the organization must feel that they are closely belonging to the organization. This attitude takes the organization to a greater height of success. Therefore, organization must strive to build corporate culture and values in the minds of the people to achieve desired goals smoothly and successfully.

9.9 CORPORATE POWER AND POLITICS

Power

Power may be defined as the capacity to a person, term, department or organization to influence others. Power has a potential to influence and change the attitude of people. Usually subordinates expect some favour from his superior. Favour may be related to work allotment, work schedule, promotions, etc.

Different types of power are:

1. **Legitimate Power:** This is the ability of the managers to use position to influence behaviour of people worming in the organization.
2. **Reward Power:** This arises due to the ability of managers to reward positive results. People are influenced to follow instruction of the executives with a pre-assumption that they will get positive outcome by following the instructions.
3. **Coercive Power:** Is the ability to apply punishment. Supervisors have power to demote and retrench employees using coercive power.
4. **Expert Power:** Some persons possess indepth knowledge and skills in certain areas. People tend to follow the instructions and influence of such people. Expert power arises due to the expert knowledge or skill possessed by an individual.

5. **Referent Power:** Is an inborn quality of a charismatic leader. These persons can influence people through interpersonal relationships. These people influence subordinates to follow their direction willfully.

Politics

To certain extent politics play significant role in an organization. Politics may be understood as the use of available power. Political behaviour of the employees cannot be completely eliminated. Political behaviour contributes to the accomplishment of organizational goals. If the management is able to use politics by regulating dysfunctional politics, better results can be seen in the organization. Following are the implication of power and politics on the behaviour and performance.

1. Executives can use power and politics to motivate the workers to achieve common goals of the organization.
2. If power and politics are used properly, it will lead to job satisfaction of the employees and to achieve higher performances.
3. Power and politics enable the executives to create an attitude of term work among the people working in the organization.
4. The referent power and expert power provides employee empowerment.
5. Employee involvement is provided by counter-power and politics.
6. Power and politics helps in moulding behaviour of unwilling workers positively and bring to a desired level.

9.10 FUNCTIONAL STRATEGIES (PLANS AND POLICIES)

Functional strategies are short-term plan for the key functional areas. They help in accomplishing annual plans. Functional strategies help organization to accomplish long-term objectives systematically. In fact, functional strategies translate grand strategy into action. Corporate strategy must be analyzed into various key functional strategies.

It is clear that functional strategies are formulated to achieve corporate objectives by maximizing the productivity of available resources. All resources strategies must align themselves with the corporate grand strategy. Well designed functional strategy system helps an organization to gain competitive advantages over its competitors.

Functional Plans and Policies

Strategy implementation involves various policy decisions including functional areas. Functional strategies direct various functions that support the corporate grand strategy. In large organizations, functional policies have to address multiple variables. For example, marketing function may have sub-functions such as, product development, advertising, sales promotion, market research, etc. Therefore, functional policy should list out all the activities relating to each functional area. Functional policies must take into consideration, the environmental impact of policy decision. It should also take into consideration the implication of resource on the functional decisions. Functional managers must keep business strategy while formulating their respective functional policy.

Need for Functional Policies

Functional policies control and reinforce corporate strategies in several ways. Designing appropriate functional strategies are significant from the following reasons:

1. Functional strategies divide corporate strategies into manageable small functions.
2. Functional managers consult each other while formulating their respective strategies. It avoids conflicts in regard to resource allocation.
3. Due to the functional strategies, proper decentralization takes place in the organization. Each functional head is free to formulate their policies within the power given to them.
4. Routine matters and ordinary problems are quickly solved by functional managers. This gives more time

to the top level executives to concentrate on strategic issues.

5. By working on the similar line day in and day out, functional managers become experts in their respective function. If all the functional areas are specialized, the entire organization gains specialization, core competence and competitive advantages.
6. Functional policies take into consideration both internal and external factors. Hence, it provides flexibility in its operation.

Financial Policies

Financial plan of an organization is concerned with the planning and controlling of financial resources of the company. Financial policy is considered as a vital and integral part of overall management. Financial plan is responsible for estimation of financial resources, their procurement and their application in a manner in which they help the enterprise to grow according to well-defined objectives. Therefore, financial plan must answer the following questions:

1. From where the company gets the required funds?
2. How and to what extend reserves and surplus be used to finance the activities?
3. What is the ratio of internal and external sources of financing?
4. What capital is desired for the development of the company?
5. What is the component of different assets that the company needs to maintain?

On the whole, financial plan takes care of three major issues

- **Sources of Funds.** Financial plan should take decision regarding the various sources of funds based on requirement, both for working capital and fixed capital. It should also mention the ratio of internal and external funding for different activities.
- **Uses of Funds.** Once the sources are identified and amount is collected, funds must be properly used.

Decision should be taken regarding capital investment, dividend decisions, etc.

- **Management of Funds.** Management of funds including accounting, budgeting, management of cash, management of credit, cost control, tax planning, etc.

Characteristics of a Sound Financial Plan

1. The plan must present a simple capital structure.
2. It should not address only the present needs but should address future need also.
3. It should ensure intensive use of available finance.
4. Financial plan must be flexible enough so that adjustment and readjustment of capital can be made based on the requirement.
5. Financial plan provide for contingencies.
6. There must be liquidity in the plan. Enough liquid assets to be maintained to meet routine requirement.
7. Cost of capital should be economical. Benefit derived should be more than the cost. It should also be noted that the investment must be made in profitable avenues.

Marketing Policies

Marketing consist of business activities that direct the flow of goods and services from producer to the final consumer. Marketing is the creative marketing function which promotes trade and employment by assessing consumer needs and initiating research and development to meet them. It coordinates the resources of production and distribution of goods and services.

Marketing policies are formulated to manage efficiently the 4Ps of marketing mix—product, price, place and promotion.

Product is the thing possessing utility. Decision regarding product mix involves product range, after sales services, brand, and packaging.

Price mix includes decision regarding pricing, discounts allowances and terms of credit. It deals with price competition.

Promotion mix includes the decision relating to advertising, personal selling, sales promotion, publicity, public relation, exhibition and demonstration, etc., largely, these activities deal with non-price competition.

Marketing policies should answer the following questions:

1. Which of the product line is required to be expanded or contracted, and to what extent?
2. Which channel will be used to market the new product?
3. How are we going to promote the new product?
4. Should the company concentrate on advertising, personal selling or other form of promotion?
5. Do we have adequate sales personal to push the product?
6. How do we answer price and non-price competition?

Operational Policies

The basic philosophy of operation management is to attack on direct costs and effectively use available resources for the production of quality goods or services for the maximum satisfaction of the customer.

Operational policies address the following four issues:

1. Product planning.
2. Supply of men, machine and materials.
3. Production control-quality and process.
4. Research and development.

The basic objective of production planning and control is to achieve maximum production efficiently by adopting appropriate process and techniques of manufacturing. It includes routing, scheduling, dispatching, inspection, coordination, and control of men, materials, machine, tools and operating time. Specific functions of production planning and control are

1. Preparation of production budget.
2. Determination of quantity and quality of machine and equipment.

3. Decision regarding manufacturing methods and process.
4. Determination and supervision of plant layout.
5. Time and motion study.
6. Determination of manpower requirement.
7. Development of new techniques of production.
8. Designing and use of quality control tools and techniques.

Research and development should be an ongoing activity in the organization. It is through this activity, the organization can develop new ideas, new product, new process, etc. Following are the questions to be answered by R&D policy.

1. Is our current R&D policy yielding desired results, or do we modify it to meet current requirement?
2. What new projects are necessary to support the growth?
3. How much should the company invest on R&D programmes?

Personnel Policies

Personnel policies deal with planning, organizing and controlling of various functions of procuring, developing, maintaining and utilizing labour force in such a way that the

(a) Objectives for which the organization is established are attained economically and effectively.

(b) Objectives of all levels of personnel are served to the highest possible degree.

(c) Objectives of the community are duly considered and served.

Personnel policies should answer the following questions:

1. Do we have an adequate workforce to carry-out our plans?
2. Do we require more hands? If yes, how many and of what quality?
3. How are we going to train and develop them?

4. Is the compensation plan just and fair?
5. Are motivational policies giving desired results?

Following are the functions of personnel policies:

- **Planning.** It is concerned with manpower planning.
- **Organizing.** It involves the provision of structure for positions and communication.
- **Directing.** It involved issuing instructions to the workers and integration of workers.
- **Controlling.** It establishes standards for job analysis, performance appraisal, etc.
- **Industrial Relations.** It covers various activities directed towards establishment of industrial peace and harmonious relationship.
- **Personnel Research and Audit.** It covers research on various techniques adopted in the organization for the benefit of the employees. It may include motivational techniques, evaluation techniques; promotion techniques, etc. personnel research helps the organization. Personnel audit ensures whether the establishment practices are followed properly.

Integration of Functional Plans and Policies

Corporate strategy is divided into various functional areas. Each functional head should formulate sound strategies and policies to accomplish their respective objectives. Strategies formulated by functional heads should not contradict the overall objectives of the organization laid down by the corporate strategy. It is therefore necessary to ensure that the functional strategies are in with the corporate strategy. It as per the schedule if there is any deviation, corrective action should be taken immediately before things go out of control.

Integration of functional strategies should take into consideration of the following:

1. Internal consistency.
2. Consideration of organizational capacity.
3. Minimize irregularity.

4. Establishing proper linkages.
5. Timing of implementation.

1. Internal Consistency. Policies formulated by functional areas must be consistent for the effective implementation of strategies. Practice and policies should not be changed more frequently. Little modification may be incorporated and policy can be fine tuned to adjust to the situation. Frequent and inconsistent functional strategies result in poor implementation of strategies. Consistency should exist in all the functional areas as they are interrelated. If one area is aggressive and others are passive, there is a tool mismatch in the policy formulation and execution.

2. Consideration of Organizational Capacity. Organization struggle hard to gain competitive advantages in the market. In order to gain competitive advantages, organization should concentrate on its core competencies and critical success factors. More resources are needed to support these variables. Organization may decide to sell quality products with competitive price. This requires efficient distribution mechanism, supported by aggressive sales promotion. Understanding of core competency helps the organization to formulate and implement suitable functional strategies.

3. Minimize Irregularity. It is a natural tendency of individuals to show domination to satisfy their needs. The same happens in the organization. Functional heads may fight for a greater share of resource for their respective departments. This may lead to frictions in the organization. Sometimes, it is necessary to sacrifice a little for the development of the organization. In order to avoid dissatisfaction, friction, etc., functional heads should consult each other and formulate strategies so that each functional area receives due consideration. Unless coordination exists, resources cannot be used optimally and strategy cannot be executed effectively.

4. Establishing Proper Linkages. Decision regarding linking different functions is desirable for the success of the strategy. Intensity of linkage must be understood for proper coordination. For example, if marketing department decides to sell low-cost customer goods, there should be greater coordination between marketing function and production/operation function. Intensity of linkage varies from time to time based on the requirements of the strategy.

5. Timing of Implementation: Timing of functional policy is vital for strategic success of an organization. Functional areas are interdependent and interrelated. Different functions cannot be undertaken in isolation. Proper blend must exist between functions. Marketing function cannot succeed without the support of production, finance and HR functions. Time for the execution of functional policies should be properly decided and executed. If the parity does not between the functions, better results cannot be expected.

9.11 PROCEDURAL IMPLEMENTATION

After the organization is satisfied with the feasibility of the project, it has to undergo certain procedures. Procedure is a regularity framework within which the management is supposed to implement its plans, project and policies as per government approval. Therefore, procedure is an inevitable and integral part of project planning. Following are the important procedures connected with a project implementation:

1. Formulation of a company.
2. Licensing procedure.
3. SEBI requirements.
4. Foreign collaboration.
5. FEMA requirements.
6. MRTP requirements.
7. Business incentives.
8. Import and export requirements.
9. Labour legislation.
10. Patenting requirements.
11. Environmental requirements.
12. Consumer protection requirements.

Formulation of a Company

Formulation brings a company into existence. Registration is an essential part of company formulation. Company should obtain certification of incorporation from Registrar of Companies.

Licensing Procedure

Licensing procedure indicates the permission to be obtained from the government. Industries Development and Regulation Act, 1951 (IDRA) provides licensing system for the industries. According to the Act, industries are divided into three categories. Industries which are under the direct control of the government are included under the first category. Second category includes those industries promoted by government and supported by private sector. All industries under private sectors are covered under third category. Secretary of industrial approval scrutinize the application for license and issue a license only if the stipulated conditions are complied with.

SEBI Requirements

SEBI Act was passed in the year 1992 to replace capital issues control Act, 1956. SEBI has three objectives, viz.

(a) Protection of the interests of investors in securities.

(b) To develop security market.

(c) To regulate securities market.

SEBI issues guidelines from time to time to supervise matters under its control. This guidelines influence those companies to collect their required funds from the capital market.

Foreign Collaboration

Foreign collaboration, in a way, partnership between home and foreign industrialists for the establishment of joint venture in the home country. It is an agreement under which industrially leading country provides machinery, technical assistance, financial assistance and so on. Expansion and diversification may need sophisticated equipment technology, huge amount of capital investment and know-how. Foreign collaboration certainly needs government approval. Government allows foreign investment and collaboration selectively.

FEMA Requirements

Foreign Exchange Management Act was introduced in the year 2000 to replace FERA. Several rules are formulated to facilitate foreign exchange by increasing Indian exports. In recent days foreign exchange transaction are increasing due to globalization. This necessitates exchange control in the country. The objective of exchange control is to regulate the demand for foreign exchange within the limits set by the available supply.

MRTP Requirements

Monopolies and Restrictive Trade Practices (MRTP) Act, 1969 aims at preventing monopolistic, unfair, restrictive trade practices and concentration of economic power in the hands of big industrialists. The Act aims at curbing price discrimination, selling goods below cost to beat competition, restricting a dealer to sell products in selected areas, restricting a dealer to sell company's product only etc. while formulating strategies, company must be careful enough to see whether the decision taken leads unfair or restriction trade practices.

Business Incentives

The central and state government offer incentives for the promotion of industries in the country. Strategies cannot ignore such incentives while formulating strategies. Some of the incentives offered by the governments are infrastructural incentives, promotional incentives, small-scale industries, incentives, backward area incentives, etc.

Import and Export Requirements

Common tendency of modern business unit is to go global. This necessitates modernization, diversification or expansion strategies. If an organization is engaged in international trade, import and export activities become a regular phenomenon. Import may involve import of capital goods, raw materials, etc. there may be restrictions on such imports. In the products from the country. Therefore, it is essential that the strategy makers understand the prevailing export and import requirement while formulating relevant strategies.

Labour Legislation

Labour constitutes a vital resource for a company. Government formulates policies to safeguard the interests of the labour. These legislative rules certainly influence strategy formulation. There are several laws related to labour working in different industries. Therefore, strategies must be aware of the labour legalization applicable to his industry and company.

Patenting Requirements

Organization will always be on the lookout continuous development and innovations. They wish to patent their products and ideas. There are formulates to be followed while patenting their products or ideas. Strategists must know the procedure and practice involved in getting patent right to the procedure and practice involved in getting patent right to the organization. In recent years patent has become more essential for some of the industries like software, chemical, pharmaceuticals, etc. It has been a proven fact that the organization with a strong patent right can gain competitive advantages more quickly than its competitors.

Environmental Requirements

While formulating strategies, one cannot ignore environment issues. Organization has got certain responsibilities towards the society in which it operates. It is expected to protect its surroundings form various pollutions like air, water, social, noise, etc. therefore, the policy makers should also formulate strategies to avoid such pollutions. It is expected from the organization that they must not conduct such business activities which are detrimental to the interest of the society.

Consumer Protection Requirements

Customers are the central focus of any activity of an organization. Organization must remember that satisfied customers bring repeated sales to the organization. Therefore it is essential to protect the interest of the customer. Organization is expected not be indulge in unethical policy makers must make sure that the policy decisions are not harmful for the interest of its customers.

9.12 PROJECT IMPLEMENTATION

Besides the completion of various regulatory formalities, strategy implementation requires project implementation. A project is a type of plan which can be thought in terms of planned actions integrated into a unity and designed to bring about a stated objective.

Depending on the nature of strategy, the size and nature of project would be determined. Thus, it can be a large-scale project involving investment of thousand of crore of rupees under expansion strategy or can be a small one involving much lesser amount like plant renovation and addition of balancing equipments under modernization strategy.

However, generally, the project is referred to investment of substantial resources. From this point of view, a project has the following characteristics:

1. Project activity is definable in terms of specific objectives. Thus, each project contributes in some way towards the realization of the organizational objectives.
2. Project activity is unique, infrequent or sometimes even unfamiliar to the organization. It is not of routine type or repetitive type and, therefore, the organization is required to take action considering all relevant factors whenever any project is undertaken.
3. Project activity is complex in respect to interdependence of various tasks accomplishments. A project contains a complex of goals, policies, procedures, rules, task assignments, steps to be taken. Resources to be employed and other elements necessary to carry out a given course of action.
4. Project activity is critical to the organization in terms of realization of its objectives. Therefore, completion of project at right time and with appropriate cost is necessary. For example, opening of factory, a project undertaken by the organization, will have certain time schedule and cost involvement. If it is delayed, there may be cost overrun. Similarly, if an

organization has undertaken project work on behalf of other organization, its completion within time limit is necessary otherwise there may be fine delay which reduces profit volume.

9.12(a) *PHASES OF A PROJECT*

A project generally, passes through five phases: conception phase, definition phase, planning and organizing phase, implementation phase, clean-up phase. At each of these phases, activities involved are quite different.

1. Conception Phase

Conception phase of a project formulation is co-existensive with strategy formulation. When an organization wants to grow through undertaking a new project, ideas are generated about which project to undertake in the light of organization's mission, its strategic intent, its business definition, its strengths and weaknesses and environmental variables. At this stage, a number of competing projects emerge which are arranged in priority on the basis of some initial criteria.

2. Definition Phase

After the conception phase is over and various projects are arranged in priority, they go through definition phase. At this phase, two types of activities are undertaken. First, there are activities related to evaluation of overall suitability of different projects in terms of marketing, technical, financial, and hoe various stakeholders particularly those who have direct financial stake in the new project would react about this. After finalizing this aspect, a detailed feasibility report is prepared about the projects which are likely to be considered for final choice. Afterwards, a project is chosen foe implementation.

3. Planning and Organizing Phase

After a project is finalized, it goes through planning and organizing phase which includes getting necessary clearances from various authorities as discussed under procedural implementation; creation of project term; arrangement of funds, infrastructure and other facilities; and drawing of schedules and procedures for project implementation.

4. Implementation Phase

This is the actual phase of project implementation. At this phase, various activities like acquisition of land, construction of factory and other premises, procurement of plant and machinery, installation of plant and machinery, etc. are undertaken. When all construction and erection work is over, testing, trial, etc. are undertaken.

5. Clean-up Phase

When the project implementation is over, clean-up phase is undertaken which includes disbanding of project infrastructure, and project term for future assignment and the project is handed over to those who run it.

9.12(b) *USE OF PERT/CPM IN PROJECT IMPLEMENTATION*

PERT (Programme Evaluation and Review Technique) was developed by the special project office of the U.S. Navy in 1958. Almost at the same time, engineers at the Du Pont Company. U.S.A., also developed CPM (Critical Path Method).

Through there is some difference between PERT and CPM, both utilize the same principles. The basic difference between the two is that CPM assumes the duration of activities is allowed and is measured by three parameters most optimistic duration, most likely duration, and most pessimistic duration.

PERT/CPM is a useful and convenient tool in the hands of a project manager who has the overall managerial responsibility of a project. Moreover, it is helpful in solving-problems of scheduling the activities of one-time projects, that is, the projects which are not taken on routine basis.

Some fields of application of PERT/CPM are the construction industry, planning and launching a new project, installing and debugging a computer system, scheduling ship construction/ repairs, missile countdown procedures, etc. It contribute in project implementation in the following ways:

It forces managers to plan because it is impossible to make time-event analysis without planning and seeing how the pieces fit together. It also forces planning at lower levels because each manager has to plan the activities for which he is responsible.

It focuses attention on critical activities because a delay in their performance will delay the whole project unless managers are able to make up the time by shortening some future activities.

It presses for right action, at right point, and at right time in the organization.

9.12(c) *PROCESS OF CPM/PERT*

A project consists of several activities and sub-activities. In order to complete the project, these activities, sub-activities should be completed in a proper sequence and in allotted time. Since some of the activities can be taken simultaneously, a network is developed to show the sequence, time taken, and the time of start of particular activities. The whole process involved in the preparation of PERT/CPM is as follow:

1. Identification of Activities

Activities represent jobs that should be performed in order to complete the programme or project. Each activity takes some specific time under given conditions.

2. Sequential Arrangement of Activities

There is always a technological sequence in the various activities of a project. Preceding and succeeding events should be located to bring the sequence. Preceding events are those which should be completed before a particular event can start. Succeeding events are those that immediately follow another event.

3. Time Estimates of Activities

All events are associated with a definite point of time and as such, events provide a basis for measuring the progress of a programme. Hence, there should be correct estimate of time taken by each activity.

However, the activities are performed in future and it may not be possible to forecast the future happening correctly, consequently the correct time estimate of activities. To overcome this problem, three time estimates are taken: optimistic time showing the least time of an activity, pessimistic time showing the maximum time of activity, and most probable time which lie in between the two. The expected time of an activity is calculated by $\frac{0+4m+p}{6}$.

4. Network Construction

All activities of a programme are connected sequentially to form a network know as PERT network. Following are rules for construction of PERT/CPM network:

(i) One and only one arrow represents each completely defined activity.

(ii) The length of the arrow does not depend upon the duration of the activity but is governed by the need for convenience and clarity.

(iii) The start or termination of an activity is represented by code or a circle.

(iv) Arrows originated at an event indicate activities that can begin only when all the activities terminating at that event have been completed.

(v) If an event takes precedence over another but there is no activity to connect them, a dummy arrow represented by dotted line is used.

(vi) Foe clarity, thick arrows or different coloured arrows are used to show critical path activities after they have been identified through analysis.

(vii) Events are distinguished by numbers. No two events can have same number. Each event, which indicates termination of an activity, has higher number than the event which indicates start of the same activity.

5. Critical Path

On the basis of analysis, critical activities are determined. These are represented by a critical path which shows that if activities on this path are not completed in time, the entire project will be delayed by the amount the event is delayed. Thus, based on estimates, the earlier or least start time of an activity can be calculated.

9.13 STRUCTURAL IMPLEMENTATION

According to Miner and Gray, "Implementation of strategies is concerned with the design and management of system to achieve the best integration of people, structures, process and resources in reaching organizational purposes".

Accomplishment of organizational goal requires collection and integration of various resources. A proper relationship must be established between various resources in the organization. Successful implementation of strategy requires support, discipline, motivation and hard work from all the people working in the organization.

Organization must distribute work among the people and fix proper responsibility and accountability for the accomplishment of the stated task within the given authority.

Therefore, there is a necessity for a suitable organizational structure. Structure is the "division of tasks for efficiency and clarity of purpose, and coordination between interdependence parts of the organization to ensure organizational effectiveness".

Strategy is influenced by several factors like the size and nature of business, market characteristics, characteristics of the strategy, etc.

The McKinsey Company, a well-known management consultancy company of United States has given a popular model known as 7-S framework for the success of the organization.

In the organization, many interrelated and interdependent activities exist. All these activities are intertwined in such a manner that if there is a change in any one of the activities, there exists cascading effect. Therefore, changing one or two variables rarely brings significant results in the organization.

7-S model advocates that whenever there is a change, there must be proper blend of these 7'S: strategy, structure, systems, style, staff, shared values, skill.

Strategy

Long-term decision aimed at gaining competitive advantage for the organization. Strategy must give scope for modification to suit environmental changes.

Structure

Shows authority and responsibility relationship between the people working at different levels. It a chart that explains who reports to whom. It clearly shows how the tasks are subdivided and integrated. Based on the change in the strategy, structure must also be altered.

System

Several activities are involved in daily operation of a business. Flow of activities should follow a system for an effective accomplishment of objectives. Proper system avoids confusion and duplication of work. Changes that are made in the structure should be incorporated in the system of operation.

Style

Leadership style adopted by the management goes a long way in attaining organizational goal. How managers act is more important than what managers say. Managers' behaviour influences the behaviour of their subordinates.

Staff

Acquiring and developing employees is vital in the organizational success. Committed workforce is an asset to the organization. They must be motivated to contribute their maximum efforts for the development of the organization. Quality and quantity of workforce should change to suit the demanding situation.

Shared Values

Beliefs, mindset and assumptions that of the organization has an impact on the overall corporate culture. Shaping the minds of people to adjust to the changed environment is more essential. It is the belief and values system that takes employees and the organization to newer heights.

Skill

Organizational capabilities and competencies help the organization to gain competitive advantages. These strong qualities must be polished and strengthened to maintain competitive advantage over a long period of time.

9.13(a) *IMPORTANCE OF ORGANIZATION STRUCTURE*

Following are the importance of the organizational:

1. It determines the nature of work to be done by different people in the organization.
2. It establishes relationship between various activities in the organization.
3. It establishes an effective communication system in the organization.
4. It ensures proper delegation of authority and responsibility.
5. It ensures smooth functioning of the organization.
6. It ensures co-operation among workers.
7. It helps effective use of human resource of the organization.
8. It encourages creativity.
9. It prevents duplication of work.
10. It helps in measuring performance of people in the organization.

9.13(b) *STRUCTURAL CONSIDERATION*

Organization structure is not a mere graphical representation of activities and people responsible for various activities. It covers various activities like:

1. Identification of different activities needed to accomplish the strategy under consideration.
2. Group the activities based on the skill required.
3. Establish proper authority and responsibility.
4. Establish effective information system and administration of the same.

5. Designing and administration of motivation.
6. Designing and administration of appraisal system.

9.13(c) *PRINCIPLES OF ORGANIZATIONAL STRUCTURE*

For the success of an organization structure, following principles are to be borne in mind:

1. Principle of Objectivity

Structure must be formulated to suit the basic objective of the organization. The structure should not contradict the basic objective.

2. Principle of Span of Control

Span of control refers to the number of persons on individual can effectively control. Span of control is based on several factors like ability, the nature of job, etc. These factors must be carefully considered before deciding the structure.

3. Principle of Exception

Only exceptional matters should be referred to the executives and the routine matters should be decided by the subordinates themselves.

4. Principle of Specialization

Functional division of activities should take place and tasks must be assigned to an individual based on his specialization to facilitate specialization.

5. The Scalar Principle

In order to make management effective, there must be clear line of authority from top to bottom.

6. Principle of Authority

Authority and responsibility should be properly matched. Responsibility is a duty and authority is the power to discharge given responsibility.

7. The Principle of Unity of Command

According to this, each subordinate should have only one supervisor and dual subordination should be avoided.

8. Principle of Delegation

Organization structure should provide for delegation of authority at every level.

9. Principle of Responsibility

According to this principle superiors are not allowed to avoid responsibility by delegating responsibilities to their subordinates. Superiors are held responsible for the acts of their subordinates.

10. Principle of Flexibility

The organization structure must be flexible so that it can be adaptable to the changing circumstances. If the structure is rigid, modification is not possible and expansion becomes difficult.

11. Principle of Simplicity

Organization structure must be simple both in its expressions and constitution. It should have minimum number of levels. People must be in a position to understand the system clearly.

12. Principle of Continuity

An organization has got perpetual existence. So long the organization exists, organization structure exists. Structure must be dynamic and should be adaptive to the changing circumstances.

13. Principle of Unity of Direction

The group acting towards the same objective must have one plan and direction. It different plans are given to different people in the group, coordination cannot be achieved.

14. Principle of Effectiveness

Structure must facilities effective functioning of the organization with minimum cost and effort.

15. Principle of Balance

Human, technical and financial factors must be properly balanced towards the accomplishment of the objectives.

9.13(d) *STRATEGIES FOR ORGANIZATION STRUCTURE*

Organization structure is formulated to suit the organizational requirement. Structure depends on various factors like the size of the organization, objectives of the business, marketing channels etc. An organization structure may undergo changes when there are changes in such factors based on which the structure is constricted.

Some if the commonly used structures are given below:

1. Entrepreneurial structure.
2. Functional structure.
3. Product based structure.
4. SBU organizational structure.
5. Geographical organization structure.
6. Matrix structure.

Entrepreneurial Structure

Very small organizations follow the structure. Decision-making power is concentrated in the hands of the owner-manager. Owner himself supervisors all the activities in the organization.

Advantages

1. Quick decision is possible as the decision-making power is centralized in the hands of owner-manager.
2. As the owner-manager himself supervises the activities, intimate relationship can be maintained with everybody in the organization.
3. Owner-manager can completely devote his time and knowledge for the absolute development of the organization.
4. The structure is simple and can easily be used by small enterprises.

Disadvantages

1. The structure becomes inadequate when organization grows.

2. Development of future managers is restricted as the decision-making is one man show.
3. Due to his concentration on supervisory work, owner-manager may not find enough time for strategic planning.

Functional Structure

Various functions performed by the organization are taken as the basis for the formulation of functional structure. Production, finance, marketing, HR and R&D are the usual functions performed by an organization.

Advantages

1. Top management can concentrate on strategic issues as functional heads taken care of respective activities.
2. It clearly defines function and responsibilities.
3. Control is made easy, as the major functions are under the direct control of the chief executive.
4. It provides specialization for the people working for a specific function.
5. It simplifies training, as training to be imparted is limited to a particular function.

Disadvantages

1. Coordination between various functional areas is very difficult.
2. It may lead to line staff conflict.
3. It provides a limited specialization as people are trained to carry out a specific function only.
4. It is not suited for an organization with many lines of business.

Product Based Structure

Under product based structure, all functions important for the production of a product or service are grouped together. The organization is split into product division. The divisional head is responsible for performance and operating decision-making. This structure is well suited for an organization with multiple products having distinct manufacturing and marketing features.

Advantages

1. The most suited structure for an organization with multiple products having distinct manufacturing and marketing features.
2. Measurement of the performance of each unit is made easy.
3. Coordination of different departments working towards a product can easily be secured.
4. Product development and market exploitation are made easy.
5. Faster decision is possible, as most of the decisions are taken at the departmental levels.
6. Responsibility for profit can be fixed at divisional levels.

Disadvantages

1. This type of structure may give rise to divisional conflicts.
2. Coordination becomes tough, if there are too many divisions.
3. As each department has all the functional areas, duplication exist in acquiring and use of resources like personnel, equipment, etc.

SBU Organizational Structure

The SBU structure is an example of the divisional structure. Each SBU operates as a separate organization. SBU is under the control of chief executive. SBU chief executive performs the roles similar to those of MD and attempts to achieve the best results in their business units within the facilities and resources provided, freedom sanctioned, and under overall corporate objectives.

Advantages

1. In-depth business planning is possible at each SBU.
2. Accountability can easily be identified at business level.
3. Well suited for an organization with distinct businesses.

Disadvantages

1. Too many SBUs may cause difficult in efficient management.
2. Assigning responsibility and accountability for SBU heads may be difficult.
3. This structure may create unhealthy competition for corporate resources.

Geographical Organization Structure

Geographic organization structure is followed by those organizations which are operating in different geographical regions. Each geographical unit has all functions required to produce and market the products in the geographical area under consideration. Each graphical head is responsible for the formulation of strategies for the accomplishment of their respective regional objectives.

Advantages

1. Needs of customers in different regions can be properly satisfied.
2. Organization can fix responsibility for each region in respect to profit etc.
3. Products can be designed to suit each geographical region.
4. Technological and legal adjustments can easily be made based on each region.

Disadvantages

1. There is a difficulty in proper coordination.
2. There is duplication of equipments and facilities.
3. Organization may not be in a position to appoint specialists due to duplication of personnel.

Matrix Structure

In large companies there are number of products and projects. Organization should ensure optimum use of available resources for the accomplishment of these projects. There must not be any shortage for resources. Also there must be any duplication in resource deployment. This can be very well solved only by matrix structure. The matrix organization structure operates on a dual channel of authority, performance, responsibility, evaluation and control. Subordinates are assigned to functional area managers as well as project/product managers. Matrix structure is a conflict resolution system through which strategic and operating priorities are negotiated, power is shared and resources are allocated internally.

Advantages

1. It has capacity of accomplishing a wide variety of project oriented business activity.
2. It helps in optimum utilization of available organizational resources.
3. It makes an organization more dynamic and result-oriented.
4. It provides opportunities for the middle-level managers to expose themselves to various strategic decisional issues.

Disadvantages

1. Dual authority system may lead to lot of confusion in the minds of people in the organization.
2. Cost and profit responsibilities many not be clear in this structure.
3. It involves greater administrative cost.

Chapter 10

Strategic Evaluation and Control

STRATEGIC EVALUATION

10.1 MEANING

Strategic evaluation is the assessment process that provides executives and managers performance information about programs, project and activities designed to meet organization goals and objectives.

10.2 DEFINITION

Evaluation of strategy is that phase of the strategic management process in which the top managers determine whether their strategic choice as implemented is meeting the objectives of the enterprise.

10.3 DIFFERENCE BETWEEN STRATEGIC AND OPERATIONAL CONTROL

Sl.No.	Attributes	Strategic control	Operational control
1.	Basic question	Are we moving in right direction?	How are we performing?
2.	Aim	Proactive, continuous questioning of the basic direction of strategy	Allocation and use of organizational resources
3.	Main concern	Steering the future direction of the organization	Action control
4.	Focus	External environment	Internal organization
5.	Time horizon	Long-term	Short-term

6.	Exercise of control	Exclusively by top management, may be through lower-level support	Mainly by executive or middle management on the direction of top management
7.	Main techniques	Environment scanning, information gathering, questioning and review	Budgets, schedules and MBO

10.4 BARRIERS OF STRATEGIC EVALUATION

We may face various constraints while evaluating strategy. Following the various barriers of strategic evaluation:

1. Psychological Barriers

- Managers are motivated to evaluate their strategies because of their psychological barriers of accepting their mistakes.
- The over consciousness of the top management may prevent the objective review of whether correct strategy is implemented.
- It may result in delay in taking correct alternative action and bring the organization at satisfaction level.

2. Lack of Direct Relationship between Performance and Rewards

- Lacking of direct relationship between performance and reward may cause a demotivation among the employees.
- Manager must be motivated to evaluate the performance and strategy at the right time.

3. Operational Problems

Even if the managers agree to evaluate the strategy the problem of strategic evaluation is not over.

Strategic evaluation is a long process, many factors are not as clear for mangers to carry on their process.

10.5 CRITERIA FOR EVALUATING STRATEGY

Following six important aspects should be looked into while evaluating strategy:

Internal Consistency

At the time of evaluating strategy, it must be evaluated to know whether the strategy formulated is consistent with organizational objectives or not. Strategy must fit into the pattern of the organization. If the strategy is different from organizational objectives, the entire effort is a wasteful affair. Therefore, it is important to evaluate this crucial factor before considering any other factors for evaluation.

Consistency with Environment

Policies formulated must suit the prevailing environment. It is known that the policies are formulated to utilize the existing environment for the best advantage of the organization. Therefore, it must be seen whether the policy helps the organization to exploit opportunities and minimize weaknesses and threats. If the strategy is not in line with the prevailing environment, organization cannot utilize their chore competencies to gain competitive edge over its competitors. Organization's success is based on how quick the organization adopts itself to the changed environment. With the existing strategy it may not be possible for the organization to face the changes that are present in the environment. Therefore, it is necessary to evaluate whether the strategy relates to the present content or not.

Appropriate Use of Organization's Resources

Strategy must be formulated in such a manner that the available organizational resource is properly used. There must not be any resource kept idle in the organization. Idle resource is an indication of efficient management. Strategy must mach opportunities and organizational resources. Activities stated by strategy must not exceed organizational resources. If this happens, stated objectives cannot be accomplished properly.

Time Horizon

Corporate level strategy broadly outlines what the organizational is meant for. To accomplish these broad objectives, each organizational unit is required to formulate their respective strategies. They are expected to prepare short-term as well as long-term strategies and to align them with the corporate strategies. Therefore, it should be evaluated whether the corporate strategy permits such divisional strategies or not.

Degree of Risk

Strategy should help organizational to minimize risk. It should be evaluated to see to what extent the strategy is capable of minimizing the risk or to bear the risk. As already discussed, strategy is formulated to combat threats and minimize the risk.

Workability

Finally, the strategy must also be evaluated to see whether the strategy is really workable and is it really contributing to the basic objectives of the organization. It must have realistic approach to the activities so that the objectives are positively accomplished.

10.6 EVALUATION AND CONTROL PROCESS

The various steps available for evaluation and control process are as under

Determine What to Measure

It is true that the organization is a group of many complex activities which are interrelated and interdependent. Top management and operational need to specify what implementation and results will be monitored and evaluated. Usually the focus will be on the most significant elements like an activity involving huge amount of expense or greater number of problems.

Establish Standards

Basically strategic evaluation is concerned with the comparison of actual performance with predetermined standards.

Therefore, fixing standards for each activity is vital for the valuation and control of strategy. Standards should be set for both intermediate and final output.

Standards must also fix tolerance limit for the acceptance of each performance. It should also be remembered here that the standards set must be reliable and achievable.

If unrealistic standards are set, performance may be negative. Control standards can be classified into quantitative and qualitative stands.

Quantitative standards express standards in physical or monitory terms. Such quantitative expressions are made for sales, production, finance, etc.

Measure Performance

Actual performance must be measured periodically. These performances must be recorded properly.

Time should also be fixed for the evaluation of performance. Fixing time for evaluation is based on several factors like scale of operation, nature of business, etc.

Compare Actual Performance with the Standard

Recorded performance must be compared with the desired results. This is the stage where the deviation in performance of each activity is identified. If the actual performance is within the acceptable limit, the measurement process stops here. Variation in performance may occur in the following three ways:

1. Actual performance matches the planned one.
2. Actual performance is better than the standard level.
3. Actual performance varies generally than the planned level.

Take Corrective Action

If actual performance is outside the acceptable tolerance limit, action must be taken to correct the deviation. Performance may be adversely affected due to a number of factors such as:

1. Wrong allocation of resources
2. Faculty organization structure
3. Inefficient leadership
4. Lack of motivation
5. Absence of proper information system
6. Improper and inefficient communication system.

Management must review whether the standards set were realistic and achievable. While fixing the standards, the organization must have taken into consideration of its capabilities. If standards are not properly set, standards may not be achieved. Therefore organization needs to upgrade its strategies, to use resource efficiently. Evaluation may also suggest the revision or re-definition of the objectives. Based on the redefinition of organizational objectives, strategies are to be redrawn. This will call for reallocation of resources.

10.7 STRATEGIC EVALUATION CONCEPT

- Boston Consulting Group (BCG Approach)
- General Electric Approach (GE)
- Shell's Directional Policy Matrix
- A.D. Little Life Cycle Approach
- M/8 Model

10.7(a) *BOSTON CONSULTING GROUP*

Bruce Henderson founded BCG in 1963 and developed the idea of portfolio management. It gives the relationship between "cash use" and "cash generations".

BCG matrix consist of two dimensions namely the rate of growth of product market and the market share in that particular market held by the firm relative to its competitor.

Market growth rate is an indicator of the attractiveness of industry and relative market share is an indicator of the firm in that industry relative to its competitors. BCG used

- Cash cow
- Problem child
- Dog
- Stars as characteristics of a portfolio of businesses

Problem Child

- Question marks/problem child are products in fast growing markets but with low market share.
- The company faces the critical questions of whether to make further investments in these businesses or to divest.

- Question marks are clearly "High Risk".
- They are at the beginning of life cycle and not yet established and they are likely to require substantial investment.

Stars

- Stars are promising product with high market share and high growth rate.
- Many stars call for substantial investment to maintain their market share in the fast growing market.
- Market position of stars remains volatile and probably highly competitive.

Cash Cow

- As the market share mature or when the market growth rate become low the "stars would become cash cow".
- Cash cows are high market share business in slow growth industries.
- It generate lot of cash, which may be used to finance the development of other business of the company

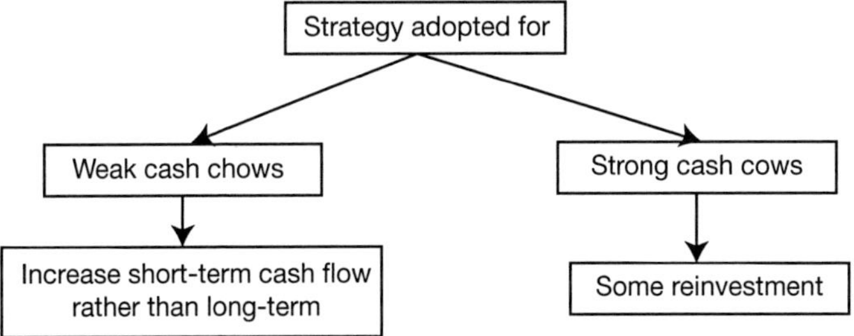

The risk is lower and the opportunity for retained earnings is high and in the case of portfolio of businesses, the corporation may be seeking to recycle such a surplus into its growth businesses.

Dogs

- Businesses with low market share in low growth industries.

- It may produce low profit/loss.
- Some dog products may have to be retained to complete the product range and provide a credible presence in the market.

10.7(b) *GE MATRIX*

McKinsey developed a GE matrix. "General Electric" started to rate its businesses on the basis of

- Business strength
- Industrial attractiveness

Each of the dimensions (industry attractiveness and business strength) is classified into three categories of high (strong), medium and low (weak), thus creating nine lines.

Every factor on each of the dimensions is assigned a weight. The choice of the factors and the weight assigned to the factors may vary from business unit to business unit.

Strategy Options using GE Matrix

Management can obtain an overall view of the corporate portfolio by placing the present and desired positions of all business units on the matrix.

Because of the scarcity of the money and other resources, the top management of most organizations must become selective and limit their investments to those business units that can provide an attractive payroll and in which they are strong.

In addition they must use some business units to finance the growth of others. Generally when a business unit is high on industry attractiveness and business strength, the strategy is to invest heavily and pursue a growth strategy.

Whenever attractiveness and business strength are low the strategy is normal to harvest or divest. In the intermediate positions, the strategy generally involves concentrating resources on the most attractive business units or in business units that have a unique competence.

Obviously the choice of what units to fund is influenced by the organizational culture and other non-quantifiable factors.

Furthermore, changes in the external factors, which can make the industry attractiveness of a business unit high, medium, or low.

		Industry attractiveness		
		High	Medium	Low
Business strengths	High	Growth	Growth	Selective Investment
	Medium	Growth	Selective Investment	Harvest or Divest
	Low	Selective Investment	Harvest or Divest	Harvest, Divest or Liquidate

10.7(c) *SHELL'S DIRECTIONAL POLICY MATRIX (DPM)*

Shell's DPM which gives market leadership concept instead of market share. Shell considered that creating a single strategic plan did not work in changing environment. It tried to develop many scenarios based on a number of assumptions about the future environment. These could be optimistic, pessimistic and straight line. Depending on the events, alternative scenarios would be used.

Shell international chemical company developed a portfolio analysis to identify the areas in which it should operate. This is called directional policy matrix (DPM). The vertical axis measures the company's present competitive position. The horizontal axis gives the prospects for portfolio operation in that sector. The criteria use dare market growth rate, market quality, feedstock and environmental aspects.

This is supposed to be better than BCG matrix as one can select criteria for different industry sector and situation.

The company's competitive position is assessed on the basis of market position, production capability and product research and development. The products with poor prospects, the suggestion is to divest and invest in faster growing areas.

- Leader box has five points. This means priority to its development.
- Try harder suggests proper resource allocation to build on a number two position.

- Quit zone or double zone suggest future prospects.
- Custodial position zone suggests that the product may fall at any time.
- Growth zone suggests allocation of resources to enable the product to grow in the market.

10.7(d) *A.D. LITTLE LIFE CYCLE APPROACH*

The life cycle approach, developed by Arthur D. Little, Inc., classifies business units within an organization by industry maturity and strategic and competitive position, resulting in the matrix.

The life cycle approach postulates that industries can be grouped into the following stages of maturity:

1. Embryonic

Characterized by rapid growth, rapid changes in technology and pursuit of new customers and fragmented and changing shares of market.

2. Growth

Characterized by rapid growth, but customer's market share, and technology are better known and entry into the industry is more difficult.

3. Mature

Characterized by stability in known customers, technology and market share. The industry can, however, still be competitive.

4. Aging

Characterized by falling demand, declining number of competitors and in many such industries, a narrowing of the product line.

The determination of a business units strategic competitive position calls for a qualitative decisions based on multiple criteria such as breadth of product line, market share, movement in market share and changes in technology.

The life cycle approach maintains that as these criteria change overtime, a business unit either gains or losses competitive advantages and can be classified as being dominant, strong, favorable and tenable or week.

10.7(e) *M/8 MODEL*

Implementing and executing strategy converting organization's strategic plan into action and then into results.

Every manager has an active role in the process executing firm's strategic plan and all employees are participants.

Management handling of the strategy implementation process can be considered successful if and when the company achieves the targeted strategic and financial performance and shows good process in realizing its long-range strategic vision.

What's worked well for some managers has been by others and found lacking. The reasons are

(i) Competitive circumstances,

(ii) Work environment,

(iii) Cultures,

(iv) Policies,

(v) Compensation incentives,

(vi) Mixes of personalities, and

(vii) Organizational histories.

The above factors require a customized approach to strategy implementation. One based on individual company situations and circumstances, the strategy-implementer's best judgment and the implementer's ability to use particular change techniques adeptly.

10.8 OPERATIONAL CONTROL

Strategic Control

A strategy is built around assumptions. These assumptions are made based on environment and organization factors which are constantly changing. Once the strategy is formulated usually it takes some time for implementation. During this interval of formulation and implementation of strategy, changes might have occurred which may affect the strategy formulated.

Therefore, strategy evaluation control plays major role in strategic management. Strategic control helps in early detection of changes in the environment.

Constant watch on environment changes is very essential for the success of the strategy and the organization. Strategy translates organization plans into action.

Strategic control provides feedback which helps in determining whether all the steps of strategic management process are appropriate, aligned with organization strategic and are performing properly.

Strategic control can be studied under the following four categories:

(i) Premise control

(ii) Implementation control

(iii) Strategic surveillance

(iv) Strategic alert control

(i) Premise Control

Strategy is formulated based on certain premise or assumption. Premise control is designed to know whether the assumption on which the strategy is formulated is still valid.

If premise itself is not valid, strategy formulated leads the organization in a wrong direction. Therefore, based on the validity or otherwise of the assumption, strategy should be altered or modified. Premise control help strategist to reject invalid premises.

(ii) Implementation Control

Implementation control aims at determining whether the strategy is properly implemented.

Implementation of strategy involves allocation of organizational resources to different activities. If implementation does not take place properly, even better strategy will fail in bringing better results to the organization.

Strategy gives broad guidelines are not properly followed, the strategy loses its significance. Strategies are altered to meet changed environment.

(iii) Strategic Surveillance

While considering strategy formulation, several factors prevailing in the environment are taken as the basis for strategy formulation. Organization might notice there are some new emerging threats in the external environment. These must be properly addressed.

For these reasons, organization must formulate strategies to combat threat. Initial detection of these reduces uncertainties and weaknesses of the organization.

(iv) Strategic Alert Control

Organization faces sudden ups and downs in its journey. These sudden changes force the organization to respond more quickly.

Government may collapse; there may be an industrial disaster. Organization must respond immediately and modify its strategy to address these changes. Organization must be ready with contingency plans to tackle these problems.

10.9 FEATURES ON AN EFFECTIVE CONTROL SYSTEM

Suitable

A single control system cannot to be applied to all the areas. The control system must be suitable to the needs of an organization. It should suit the nature and needs of the nature and needs of the area to be controlled. Therefore, control system for production and sales department must be different, as the function and nature of these departments are different.

Simple

The control system should be easily understandable to the people who use it. Complicated system will create confusion and frustration among employees. If the control systems are properly understood by the people, employees implement in the right direction.

Selective

While formulating strategies, organization should focus on key and important factors. If these factors are systematically addressed, the other areas can be managed without much difficulty.

Economical

While formulating a strategy, organization should understand whether the strategy is economical or not. Benefit derived must be more than the cost incurred.

Flexible

Organization exists in ever changing environment. Technological, competitive and other environmental changes force the organization to modify their plans. Therefore, strategic control must provide scope for flexibility. It must be flexible enough so that the policies can be modified to adjust to the changed environment.

Reasonable

Control system must be reasonable enough. It must be attainable. It should not be too high or unreasonable. In reasonable system does not motivate employees. On the other hand, if the controls are set at low levels, people may feel that these controls are not challenging.

Forward-looking

The system established must provide timely information regarding any deviation. Early detection of these deviations help managers to take necessary steps to correct them before things go out of control.

Responsibility

control system must clearly mention the person responsibility for the deviations, if any control system must also state what corrective actions are to be taken so that actual performance is in line with the desired performance.

Objective

Control system must have an objective behind its introduction. Objective must be clear and there must not be any ambiguity in its expression.

10.10 EVALUATION TECHNIQUES FOR OPERATIONAL CONTROL

Following are the most commonly used techniques for evaluating operational strategies:

- Value chain analysis
- Bench-marking
- Balanced score-card
- Quantitative performance measures
- Qualitative performance measures
- Key factor rating

Value Chain Analysis

Value chain analysis helps in understanding organization's resources and capabilities. It an organization different activities are conducted to accomplish its objectives.

Each activity consumes organizational resources. By consuming resources, it is expected that each activity should add some value to the overall accomplishment.

Activity based costing (ABC) is widely used to analyze value chain. It explains cost structure of the activities. If the organization is conducting unproductive and unwanted activities, organization loses its precious scarce resource which otherwise could have been used for productive purposes.

Value chain helps organization to improve their capabilities to attain competitive advantage by using resources for a better cause.

Bench-marking

Bench-marking is "the continuous process of measuring product, services and practices against the toughest competitors or those companies recognized as industry leaders".

Bench-marking helps in identifying the ways of improving organizational activities. Using this method evaluation can be done continuously till it reaches the best practice level. It helps the organization to see continuous and stable improvement in it.

Organization can attain competitive advantage when it out performs its competitors.

Bench-marking process involves the following steps:

- Identify the area or process to be examined.
- Obtain measurement of the process or area.
- Select industry leader/s.
- Calculate difference in the performance of the company with the industry leader/s.
- Formulate programmes to reduce the performance gap.
- Implement the programme.
- Measure and compare the new results with the selected industry leader/s.

Balanced Score-Card

Instead of considering only financial performance to evaluate the strategy, this method advocates consideration of four important key performance measures. These factors are based on customer perspective, internal business, innovation and learning perspective, and financial perspective.

(a) *Customer Perspective*

Evaluating the company from customer perspective explains the company hoe customers see the organization. This helps in understanding whether the organization stands in the minds of the customers.

If the customer's perception is good towards the company, the necessary steps are needed to maintain the same positive perception. If customer's perception is not that acceptable, suitable actions are to be taken to restore positive perception in the minds of the customers.

(b) *Internal Business Perspective*

The evaluation explains internal capabilities of the organization expressed in terms of core competencies. Organization can excel well if these core competencies are properly utilized. Proper exploitation of core competencies leads to organization competitiveness.

(c) *Innovation and Learning Perspective*

Organization must be innovative in nature. Continuous innovation helps organization to improve product, service, process and practices that are exist in the organization. Innovation helps organization to expand its customer base. Innovation also helps in work simplification, quality improvement and cost reduction.

People working in the organization must have an attitude of learning new things. This is through process one can learn new things. Learning changes the behaviour of individuals working in the organization. Learning makes an individual to adjust to the changing environment. Learning should be an ongoing phenomenon in the organization.

(d) *Financial Perspective*

This is the most common method for evaluating the performance of the strategy. It is expected that the organization should maintain steady growth in terms of profit. Ultimate aim of financial management is to maximize the wealth of the shareholders. Therefore, evaluation should analyze whether the company is catering to this need or not.

Quantitative Performance Measures

Ratio analysis is commonly used for quantitative performance evaluation. Return on investment, return on equity, profit margin, market share, debt to equity, earnings per share, sales growth, asset growth, etc., are also used for quantitative measures. The actual performance should be compared with predetermined standards periodically. There may be standards for time, cost, productivity and revenue.

Qualitative Performance Measures

Following qualitative consideration are to be considered for qualitative measure:

- Internal consistency of strategy
- Consistency of strategy with environment
- Appropriateness of strategy in view of available resources
- Degree of acceptability of the strategy

- Time horizon of the strategy
- Workability of the strategy
- Balance of invest between high-risk and low-risk project
- Social responsibility coverage of the strategy

Key Factor Rating

Key factors are those factors which influence the overall organization capability. Therefore, it is essential to keep track of key factors contributing to the success of the organization. Continuously these factors should be monitored to know where these factors hold good even in the present environment.

10.11 GUIDELINES FOR PROPER CONTROL

The following guidelines are to be followed to ensure a proper control for the evaluation of the strategy:

1. Minimum Information

Control system should involve minimum amount of information as too much of information creates confusion. It is advised to follow 80:20 rule. This rule advocates monitoring those 20% of the factors that determine 80% of the results.

2. Measurement of only Meaningful Activities

Organization should measure only meaningful activities even if it is difficult to measure the performance of these activities.

3. Timely Control

Control should be exercised timely so that corrective action can be taken quickly. Therefore constant and close monitoring of the performance of the activities of the organization.

4. Balanced Use of Long-term and Short-term Controls

There are both short-term and long-term strategies. Based on the type of strategies, control system should be formulated so that balanced control system will emerge.

5. Pinpointing Exception

Most of the time actual performance differs from the predetermined standard performance. But it should be noted here that only those results that fall outside a predetermined tolerance limit should be called for corrective action.

6. Reward System

Instead of concentrating only on punishment for poor performance, it is advised to give due consideration even for exceptional performances. Those who perform exceedingly well must be rewarded so as to creative motivational spirits in the minds of the people to perform for the accomplishment of the organizational objectives.

10.12 CHARACTERISTICS OF MANAGEMENT CONTROL

1. It is an Essential Function of Every Manager

Management control is a function exercised by every manager at all the levels of the organization. The nature and scope of control varies based on managerial level. It is also governed by the authority and responsibility of management. Without exercising control, a manager cannot do the complete job of managing.

Organization is a set of activities. All these activities cannot be carried out by manager alone. He delegates authority to his subordinates for the smooth functioning of the operations. Therefore, managers must have control over his subordinates whenever he delegates authority to his subordinates.

2. Planning and Management Controls are Closely Related

Managerial planning seeks consistent, integrated and clearly expressed programmes to accomplish predetermined objectives. Managerial control seeks to compel events to confirm to plan. As a matter of fact, planning is based on plan. This results in revision of planning setting, improving staffing and making major changes in the techniques of directing.

3. Management Control is a Continuous Activity

Management control is a continuous activity; it exists till the death of the organization. So long as the organization exists.

Continuous application of control wherever and whenever necessary, helps organization in early detection of deviation and taking corrective action. Timely corrective action brings activities into a desired level of performance. Continuous monitoring helps in continuous improvement of the organization which puts organization into a competitive position in the market.

4. Management Control is Forward Looking

Management control is forward looking because it is on the basis of evaluation of the past performance, the future guidelines are formulated. It highlights the past deviations and action plans are prepared to avoid recurrence of these deviations. Management control prepares the organization to face the future systematically.

5. Management Controls People-Oriented

Organization is group of people working towards the accomplishment of the common objective of the organization. Most of the time deviations occur due to human errors. Therefore, it is essential to apply control over the people working in the organization. These controls are prepared by human beings to control performance of people working in it.

6. Management Control is Dynamic

It involves continuous review of standards of performance based on the changed environment. The changes in standards result in the functional changes in the organization.

10.13 SCOPE OF AREAS OF MANAGERIAL CONTROL

The scope of managerial control is very wide. It virtually covers all the areas of business, namely policies, procedures, men, money, machines and equipment, public relation, human relation, research and development and so on.

Normally, managerial control is exercised by concentration on key areas of business on which the success of the business depends. It is known as "key-point control". The key-points vary from enterprise to enterprise.

The scope and the main areas of managerial control are as follows:

1. Managerial Control over Policies

The success of any organization is largely dependent on the implementation of the policies. Therefore, it is necessary to see that the policies are properly implemented. Policies do not carry any value if they are not implemented properly.

Therefore, in the whole process of strategic management properly therefore in the whole process of strategic management, implementation of policy is critical for the success of the organization. Policies are controlled through policy manual.

2. Control over Organization

As mentioned earlier, organization is a group of activities and people. Proper organizational structure must be created to accomplish organizational objectives. Proper authority and responsibility relationship should be established for proper accountability. Organization structure must be modified to suit the situation.

Traditional organization structure was tall/vertical with number of managerial levels and smaller span of control. Today we have horizontal/flat organizational structure with lesser number of managerial levels and wider span of control. Therefore, it is necessary design suits the desired requirement.

3. Control over Personnel

Organization is a group of people working towards the accomplishment of common goal of the organization. They will have their own personnel goal along with the organizational goals.

They should have prior importance to the organizational goals. If they assign more importance to their personal goals, goal conflicts arise. Therefore, it should be ensured that the people working in the organization exhibit desired behaviour in the organization and they follow rules and regulations laid down by the organization. It must also be ensured that every cross their authority limits and discharge responsibility for the good of the organization.

4. Control over Costs

Management must ensure optimum utilization of organizational resources. There must not be any unnecessary wastage of organizational resources. Therefore, cost control is exercised by setting cost standards for material, labour and overheads.

Actual cost data must be compared with the standards. If cost of operation is not under control, cost of product or service will increase. The product may not be affordable for the customers and hence the product may have to face lot of competition in the market. Cost control, therefore aims at reducing cost of operation, work simplification, reduced wastage and the like to increase profitability of the organization and to produce products at an affordable price with superior quality.

5. Control over Methods

Method adopted for performing an activity influences to a greater extent on the efficiently and effectiveness of the employees. Therefore, it is very essential to evaluate the methods adopted by each employee to identify unnecessary activity or motion if any.

By avoiding unnecessary activities it is possible not only to save organizational resources but also improve productivity of the employees. Therefore, it is necessary to exercise control over the methods adopted to perform each activity.

6. Control over Wages and Salaries

Satisfaction of people working in the organization is a vital factor for the success of an organization. Salary paid to the employees must match the standard of living of the employees. Therefore salary package must be reasonable.

Remuneration should involve different components in it. Salary should be revised based on various factors including performance and job evaluation. Once the norms are set, they should be followed without any partiality.

7. Control over Capital Expenditure

Organizations think of expanding its activities by investing an additional amount on capital assets. Capital budget helps in proper evaluation of different alternatives before investment is made capital assets. Capital expenditure must be evaluated under the lights of cost of capital, expected revenue, technology needed etc. Capital should be needed meticulously evaluated as the decision once taken is irreversible in nature.

8. Control over Production

Organization can survive only if it is capable of manufacturing products needed by its customers or rendering desired services. Buying habits of customers change. New demands may arise. Therefore, organization must understand the market needs and the attitude of customers.

Organization must decide carefully on product line and mix. Volume of production should be based on the market demand. Routing, scheduling, dispatching, inventory control, inspection and quality control are some of the popular methods adopted for production control.

9. Control over External Relations

Organization does not exist in vacuum. It exists within external environment. Therefore, it is vital that organization maintains good public relationships.

10. Control over Research and Development

Research and development activities help organization in developing new products and process. Through R&D it is possible for the organization to develop improved methods of production and work simplification.

Establishment of R&D department involves huge amount of investment. Therefore, it is essential to see the department is functioning towards the development of new ideas or product which will give competitive advantage to the company.

11. Information Control

Information is a vital resource of an organization in this competitive business world. Information is power. Information delayed is information denied. Therefore, organization must have well organized information system.

Information supplied by this system must not be accurate, adequate, timely, relevant and reliable. There must not be any ambiguity or exaggeration in the information supplied by the system.

12. Overall Control

Organizational success is possible only if all the activities are carried out in the same direction as it was desired. Therefore, it is essential that the overall control should be exercised for the overall development of the organization. This is made possible through budgetary control.

Master plan is prepared for overall control and all the departments are involved in it. Active support of top management is essential for an effective control through master plan.

10.14 TECHNIQUES OF STRATEGIC EVALUATION AND CONTROL

Strategic control is the process of taking into accounts the changing assumptions, both external and internal to the organization, on which the strategy is based, continually evaluating the strategy as it is being implemented and taking corrective actions to adjust the strategy to the new requirements. There four types of strategic controls:

1. Premise control
2. Implementation control
3. Strategic surveillance
4. Special alert control

Premise Control

Premise control is designed to check systematically and continuously whether or not the premises set during strategy formulation and implementation process are still valid.

Premises are the anticipated environment in which a strategy is expected to operate. They include assumptions of forecast of the future and known conditions that affect the operation of a strategy. If these premises are not valid, a change in the strategy is required to make it effective.

Environmental Factors

General environmental factors—economic, political-legal, technological, and socio-cultural—affect the operation of business organization. Any vital change in these factors between the times of strategy formulation necessitates change in strategy.

Industry Factors

Industry factors affect the operation of a business organization directly. While chalking strategy, every organization makes assumptions about industry structure and nature of competition in it. Any change in these factors requires corresponding change in industry.

For effective premise control, an organization may proceed in the following ways:

1. Identify the key premises which are of vital importance to strategy implementation. In fact, many of these premises are identified at the level of strategy formulation. However, nature of their change might have not been evaluated. Therefore, those premises which are likely to change must be selected for monitoring.
2. People in the organization that are likely to have access to the relevant information about premises. For example, sales force or marketing research department should be assigned the job of monitoring competitors move.
3. Ascertain trigger point at which a change in strategy is required. A trigger point is a characteristic of a situation which necessitates change in strategy. For example, in the case of a new product launch. If competitor's move, particularly the one having substantial strength, is offensive, the strategy may be changed from head-on competition to indirect competition by changing product positioning.

Strategic Momentum Control

Strategic momentum control techniques are suitable for organizations operating in a relatively stable environment. Since the environment is stable, major assumptions made at the time of strategy formulation remain valid for a long time. Though there may be change in environmental factors, such a change is gradual and on predicted lines. Thomas has suggested three approaches for strategic momentum control: responsibility control centers, underlying success factors, and generic strategies.

1. Responsibility control centers are the core of management control systems. Such centers are created on the basis of control criteria used and termed as revenue, expenses, profit, and investment centers.
2. Key success criteria enable an organization to focus on these factors. By focusing continuously on these factors, the organization can achieve its objectives.
3. Generic strategies approach to strategic control is based on the assumptions that an organization's strategy should be comparable with others in the same industry. Based on this comparison, the organization can adjust its strategy.

Strategic Leap Control

When the environment is relatively unstable and turbulent in which various factors change beyond prediction, strategic leap control is suitable. Strategic leap control helps organizations operating in such an environment in defining new strategic requirements and to cope with emerging environmental realities. There are three techniques for exercising strategic leap control: strategic issue management, strategic field analysis, and systems modeling.

1. Strategic issue management involves identifying strategic issues and assessing their impact on the organization. A strategic issue is any development, either inside or outside the organization, which has significant impact on the ability of the organization to achieve its objectives. By managing strategic issues well in time, the organization can avoid the adverse impact of environmental surprise.
2. Strategic field analysis involves examining the nature and extent of synergies that exist or that can be

developed in changing environment. By taking the advantages of its existing synergies or of those that can be developed, the organization can move towards achieving its objectives.

3. Systems modeling are simulated techniques of decision-making in which various organizational features and environmental scenarios are analyzed on simulated basis. Different scenarios to help the organization in taking appropriate strategic actions on proactive basis.

Implementation Control

Implementation control is designed to assess whether the overall strategy should be changed in the light of unfolding events and results associated with incremental steps and actions that implement the overall strategy. Several types of actions are required in implementing a strategy such as projects, programmers, resource allocation, functional strategy-related activities, behavioral problems, etc. All these actions take place incrementally over the period of time. Implementation control is undertaken in thee contexts. In designing implementation control, two aspects are taken into account: monitoring strategic thrusts and milestone review.

Monitoring Strategic Thrusts

For implementing the strategy, actions are divided into several identifiable new thrusts, that is, specific narrow actions that represent part of what needs to be done if the overall strategy is to be implemented. These trusts provide information which can be used as basis for subsequent actions. For example, for introducing a totally new product, the usual thrusts are concept development, product development, test marketing, and product launch. At each of the first three stages, information is generated which can be abandoned or product features may detoxified to make the product acceptable.

Milestone Review

Milestone is an identifiable segment of a strategy which may be in the form of critical events, major resources allocation, or simply a passage of a certain amount of timer. Each milestone requires critical assessment in terms of time and cost. For example in a project implementation, it is broken into several milestones and each of them is undertaken in either specific sequence or simultaneously with others depending on the nature of its dependence on others. Cost and time involved in completing each milestone are identified to ensure project completion within stipulated time and cost. This is somewhat similar to PERT/CPM, albeit at a smaller scale.

Strategic Surveillance

Strategic surveillance is non-focused control a dies designed to monitor a broad range of events inside and outside the organization that are likely to threaten the course of the strategy. The basic idea behind strategic surveillance is that some form of general monitoring of multiple information sources should be encouraged with the objective to uncover unanticipated yet important opportunity.

Special Alert Control

Special alert control is really a subset of other three types of control and is undertaken to access the impact of any major environmental event. Such an event may be in the form of technological invention making the present technology completely obsolete, war between two or more countries affecting the business prospects, strategic actions taken by a country or countries together controlling some critical resources like the sudden increase in petro-product prices by OPEC in 1973, and so on. Such an occurrence should trigger an immediate and intense reassessment of the organization's strategy.

Characteristics of Four Types of Strategic Control

Basic characteristics	Premise control	Implementation control	Strategic surveillance	Special alert control
Degree of focusing	High	High	Low	High
Data acquisition:				
Formalization	Medium	High	Low	High
centralization	Low	Medium	Low	High

(Contd...)

Use with:				
Environmental factors	Yes	Seldom	Yes	Yes
Industry factors	Yes	Seldom	Yes	Yes
Strategy-specific factors	No	Yes	Seldom	Yes
Firm-specific factors	No	Yes	Seldom	Seldom

10.15 FINANCIAL PERFORMANCE CONTROL

Financial performance control, or simply referred to as financial control, is relevant for those aspects of business operations whose outcomes are expressed in monetary terms. Financial control is exercised at operative level as well as at overall organization level though techniques involved are different. Financial control techniques are grouped into three categories from strategic management point of view:

1. Budgetary control,
2. Financial ratio analysis, and
3. Return on investment.

10.15(a) *BUDGETARY CONTROL*

Budgetary control is derived from the concept and use of budgets. A budget is the financial expression of various organizational operations and the way in which budgets are prepared as tools for planning. Thus budgetary control is a system which uses budgets as a means for planning and controlling entire aspects of organizational activities or parts thereof. Terry has defined budgetary control as follows:

> Budgetary control is a process of comparing the actual results with the corresponding budget data in order to approve accomplishment or to remedy differences by either adjusting the budget estimates or correcting the cause of the difference.

However the scope of budgetary control extends beyond cost control with the introduction of several types of budgeting.

On the basis of definition of budgetary control, its features can be identified as follows:

1. Budgetary control establishes a plan or target of performance which becomes the basis of measuring progression of activities in the organization.
2. It tries to measure the outcomes of activities in quantified terms so that actual performance can be compared with budgeted performance.
3. It tries to focus attention of the management on deviation between what is planned and what is being achieved so that necessary actions are taken to correct the situation and to achieve the objectives of the activities. Thus, it does not control the activities directly but points out where control and corrective actions required.

10.15(b) *FINANCIAL RATIO ANALYSIS*

Financial ratio analysis identifies the relationship between two financial variables in order to derive meaningful conclusion about their behavior. Metcalf and Tigard have defined financial ration analysis as "a process of evaluating relationship between component parts of financial statements to obtain a better understanding of a firm's position and performance "the type of relationship to be investigated depends on the objective and purpose of evaluation. In the case of measurement of overall performance, generally, four groups of ratios are considered: liquidity ratios, leverage ratios and profitability ratios. A brief description of these ratios is presented here.

Liquidity Ratios

Liquidity ratios indicate the organizations ability to pay its short-term debts. These ratios are generally expressed in two forms: current ratio and quick ratio. Current ratio shows the relationship between current assets and current liabilities. This indicates the extent to which current assets are adequate to pay current liabilities. Quick ratio indicates the relationship between liquid assets (cash in hand with bank and short-term debtors) and current liabilities. It helps in identifying without considering inventory in hand.

Activity Ratios

Activity ratios show how funds of the organization are being used. These ratios are in the form of inventory turnover ratio, receivable turnover ratio and assets turnover ratio, inventory turnover ratio indicates the number of times inventory is replaced during the year and shows how promptly the organization is able to collect dues from its debtors. Assets turnover ratio indicates how effectively assets have been used to generate sales.

Leverage Ratios

Leverage ratios indicate the relative amount of funds in the business supplied by creditors/financiers and shareholders/ owners. These ratios are in the form of debt-equity ratio, total capital ratio, and interest coverage ratio. Debt equity ratio indicates the proportion of debt in relation to equity and indicates the financial strength of the organization. Debt total capital ratio shows the proportion of debt to total capital employed. This also indicates burden being borne by the organization in relation to its profit.

Profitability Ratios

Profitability ratios show the ability of an organization to earn profit in relation to its sales and/or investment. Profitability ratios are expressed in terms of profit margin as well as return on investment. Profit margin, net profit or gross profit, is expressed in the form of relationship between profit and sales and indicates the degree of profitability of the business. Return on investment is measured by relating profit to investment. Return on investment is the most comprehensive technique for controlling overall performance. Therefore, somewhat more elaborate discussion is presented.

10.15(c) *RETURN ON INVESTMENT*

The efficiency of an organization is judged by the amount of profit it earns in relation to the size of its investment. Popularly known as Return On Investment (ROI).

This technique does not emphasis absolute profit for judging the efficiency of an organization as a whole or a division of rather the amount of profit is related with the amount of facilities or capital invested in the organization or the division. The goal of a business accordingly is not to optimize profit, but to optimize returns on capital invested for business purpose. This standard recognizes the fundamental fact that capital is a critical factor in almost any business and its scarcity puts limit on progress.

The rate of return is calculated by dividing the profit by total investment. It can be computed in respect of historical data so as to reveal the rate of return realized or it may be applied to budgeted data to give a projected rate of return. In the Du Pont system the investment includes total fixed and current assets without reducing liabilities or reserves. The basis is that such a reduction would result in fluctuations in operating investments as liabilities or reserves fluctuate, which would distort the rate of investment and render it meaningless.

10.16 SOCIAL PERFORMANCE CONTROL

Most of the organization set their social objectives either explicitly or implicitly depending on organizational practices. Social performance control deals with assessing the extent to which an organization is achieving its social objectives. This requires defining the basis on which social performance should be evaluated and identifying the degree to which social performance is effective. Thus, social performance control involves two aspects:

1. Approaches for measuring social performance
2. Social audit

10.16(a) *APPROACHES FOR MEASURING SOCIAL PERFORMANCE*

Measurement of social performance is quite fluid because of its qualitative nature. In order to overcome the problem of fluidity, a separate branch of accounting, known as social accounting, has been developed. Robert Elliot has defined social accounting, as "systematic assessment and reporting on those parts of a company's activities that have a social impact—the impact of corporate decisions on environmental pollution, consumption of non-renewable resources, and ecological factors: the rights of individuals and groups; maintenance of public service; health, safety, education and many other social concerns. In social accounting, three approaches are used for measuring social performance:

1. Social cost-benefit analysis,
2. Social indicators, and
3. Social goal setting.

Social Cost-benefit Analysis

Social cost-benefit analysis is based on evaluating benefits that accrue to the society and the costs through which these benefits accrue. While costs can be measured in terms of money, same is not the case with benefits. Since social benefits cannot be defined in monetary term, the concept of consumer surplus is applied to measure these consumer surplus is the difference between what a consumer would be willing to pay for a given product or service and the actual price charged.

Thus, this willing price may be used for measuring social benefits. However, the willing price to be paid by a consumer is subjective and varies from situation to situation for the same consumer or may be interpreted differently by various persons. For example, what is the willing price to be paid by a consumer for a packet of food, earthquake, etc.

Cost-benefit analysis may be undertaken either on the existing price system or discounted rate of costs and benefits. In the latter case, social costs and benefits are discounted at social discount rate to determine the present value of net social benefits. Social-cost benefit analysis, though suffers from the limitation of precise measurement, and is useful in evaluating the alternative social programmes that an organization can undertake.

Social Indicators

Social indicators approach of social performance measurement consists of developing social indicators and measuring an organizations performance on these indicators. Brume has prescribed five broad indicators in which the contribution of an organization should be measured. These are as follows:

1. Net income contribution—earning enough to provide for the present and future costs of the organizations continued existence but limited to legitimate socially desirable profit.
2. Human resource contribution—development of system of human resource accounting to measure the impact of the organizational decisions on human asset value.
3. Creation of jobs and providing employment opportunities to backward and handicapped population, contributing towards educational development, relief of people in distress caused by natural calamities, rural upliftment, etc.
4. Environmental contribution—environmental improvement through pollution abatement, conservation of scarce natural resources, and maintenance of ecological balance, and so on.
5. Product or service contribution—ensuring quality, safety and serviceability of products; customer satisfaction, truthfulness in advertising etc.

Social indicators approach measures social performance of an organization in the context of various factors. Many organizations follow this approach because it indicates the areas in which they have to work. However, one basic problem in this approach is the determination of expectations of various indicators and the way it can be fulfilled.

Social Goal Setting

Social goal setting approach emphasizes on incorporating social concern in the objectives of an organization which may be on a perpetual basis or on periodic basis. A combination of both can also be followed in which some social concern can be undertaken on perpetual basis while others can be taken on project basis for specific period. For example, consumer satisfaction, environmental protection, etc. can be taken on perpetual basis while special projects for certain specific social cause like eliminating the impact of destruction caused by certain natural calamities can be taken on ad hoc basis. In the social goal setting approach, an organization can identify the social concerns to be served on the basis of its own environmental analysis and choose those areas in which it believes it can contribute effectively by reducing the social costs or enhancing social benefits. This approach is better in terms of providing areas of social concerns on which the organization can focus in terms of the needs of the areas and its own capability to satisfy those needs, thus this approach can be well integrated with strategic management process.

10.16(b) *SOCIAL AUDIT*

When an organization undertakes social activities, it must also evaluate the extent to which these activities are performed effectively. Social audit is primarily aimed to measure the effectiveness of these activities. Bauer and Fen have defined social audit as follows:

> Social audit is a commitment to a systematic of and reporting on some meaningful, definable domain of the company's activities that have social impact.

Problems in Social Audit

The idea of social responsibility of which social audit is a means of measurement is quite valid in business world and it has been recognized that business organization have to fulfill their social obligations in their own long-term interests. Social audit is equally logical. Social audit, however presents numerous problems. These problems are of two types: determine scope for social audit and measurement problem.

1. Scope of the Social Audit. If a social audit is to be made, the basic question is what activities should be covered. There may be various alternatives. First, all social activities being performed by an organization may be taken for reporting. However, if the social audit is to catalogue all such activities, verify the costs involved and evaluate the benefits produced. It is very impractical to carry on the social audit and information may be too massive to be useful. The activities may be too large because it is very difficult to say which alternative are not social. Thus various activities which an organization performs are social benefits decides benefiting the organization as well. Second the various activities of clear social utility without prospect of profit may be taken into consideration. However, if only such activities are taken into account, the scope of social audit will be too limited to demonstrate the extent to which the organizations social performance is fulfilled. The scope of social audit may be determined keeping in view the information requirements of various groups such as, employees, customers, shareholders, general public and those who influence the shaping of public opinions.

2. Measurement Problems. Another major problem in social audit is related to the determination of yardsticks for measuring the costs and accomplishments of activities included in the social audit. Though costs can be measured easily, these may not be the result of social activity. Moreover how much an activity is benefiting to the society and to the organization concerned is difficult to measure. It happens that an activity may contribute to both the society and the organization.